SUPER
BUG

Author John Woodward

Consultant Dr George McGavin

DK

SUPER
BUG

CONTENTS

Senior Art Editor Smiljka Surla
Senior Editor Shaila Brown
Editors Ann Baggaley, Andrea Mills
Designers Tessa Jordens,
Tannishtha Chakraborty,
Samantha Richiardi

Managing Editor Paula Regan
Managing Art Editor Owen Peyton Jones
Producer, Pre-Production Jacqueline Street
Senior Producer Mary Slater
Jacket Design Development Manager
Sophia MTT
Jacket Editor Claire Gell
Jacket Designer Mark Cavanagh,
Suhita Dharamjit
Senior DTP Jacket Designer
Harish Aggarwal
Picture Research Manager Taiyaba Khatoon
Picture Researcher Sakshi Saluja
Publisher Andrew Macintyre
Art Director Karen Self
Associate Publishing Director Liz Wheeler
Design Director Stuart Jackman
Publishing Director Jonathan Metcalf

Illustrator Arran Lewis

First published in Great Britain in 2016 by
Dorling Kindersley Limited
80 Strand, London, WC2R 0RL

Copyright © 2016 Dorling Kindersley Limited
A Penguin Random House Company

10 9 8 7 6 5 4 3 2 1
001–283975–April/2016

A CIP catalogue record for this book
is available from the British Library.

ISBN: 978-0-2412-2847-0

Printed and bound in China

A WORLD OF IDEAS:
SEE ALL THERE IS TO KNOW

www.dk.com

SUCCESS STORY

The world is full of animals of all shapes and sizes. It's the larger mammals, birds, reptiles, amphibians, and fish that we mostly notice, but these animals are vastly outnumbered by much smaller creatures including insects and spiders. We call them bugs. Many are tiny, yet they are the most successful creatures on Earth. Insects were also the first animals to fly, enabling them to escape from predators and conquer new areas in the search for food and a mate.

SET IN STONE

Fossils preserved in rocks show that some of the bugs that live around us have changed very little over hundreds of millions of years. Insects such as dragonflies were flourishing long before the giant dinosaurs appeared, and survived the catastrophe that destroyed them. Few other types of animals have been so successful.

Giant ancestor

Found in China, this amazingly detailed fossil preserves an impression of a dragonfly. It lived 130 million years ago, and would have flown around the heads of giant dinosaurs, but it is almost identical to many dragonflies that live around us today.

Spider's leg structure is just like that of spiders living today.

AMBER AMBUSH

Sticky resin oozing from tree bark in the distant past trapped many small animals. Over millions of years, the resin turned to hard amber, preserving the trapped bugs complete with their legs, wings, mouthparts, and even internal organs. Such amazing fossils show that all the main types of bug were alive about 90 million years ago.

Showcase spider

Every detail of this spider has been perfectly preserved for millions of years by the rock-hard amber. Since the amber is transparent, scientists can see through it to identify the animal's features, and observe the similarities with modern spiders.

INDISPENSABLE INSECTS

Many people do not like bugs, and are even scared of them. It is true that some bugs bite, sting, or transmit disease, and a few can be deadly. But for millions of years they have been a vital food source for animals like this bee-eater. They are also essential flower pollinators, and without them, many plants – including some that we rely on for food – could not exist.

Long wings of this ancient dragonfly had the same structure as those of modern insects.

SMALL WONDERS

Many bugs flash with brilliant rainbow colours, and their hard external skeletons can be moulded into extraordinary shapes. Some are tiny, while others are much bigger than you would imagine possible. Their lifestyles can be astonishing and a few species are seriously dangerous. They really are superbugs.

BIRD DROPPING SPIDER
This tropical spider is camouflaged to look like a bird dropping – ensuring that no bird will try to eat it.

OAK TREEHOPPERS
Both the adult (left) and young of this sap-sucking bug have beautifully sculptured, colourful bodies.

VAPOURER MOTH CATERPILLARS
Like most bugs, this moth can multiply fast, laying hundreds of eggs that hatch as tiny caterpillars.

GIRAFFE WEEVIL
Some bugs, such as this male giraffe weevil, have evolved extraordinary features to attract a mate.

WHAT IS A BUG?

Ninety-seven per cent of all species on Earth are invertebrates – animals without backbones. Some are soft-bodied creatures such as worms, but most are animals called arthropods, which have tough external skeletons and jointed legs. We call these animals bugs. Their bodies are very different from ours, but they still need to move, eat, breathe, and sense their surroundings.

INSIDE A WASP

A wasp is a type of insect – the largest group of arthropods. All adult insects have the same basic body with three body sections, three pairs of jointed legs, and usually two pairs of wings. Their internal organs have the same functions as those of other animals – although a wasp also has a sharp sting.

VISION AND EATING

Just like us, bugs need to find their way around and eat their food. But they have developed very different tools for the job. Adult insects have eyes with hundreds of lenses, and spiders have venomous fangs.

COMPOUND EYES
This insect has compound eyes made up of many tiny elements, each with its own lens. It also has a cluster of three simple eyes on the forehead.

DEADLY JAWS
Bugs have varied types of mouthparts. This spider has strong jaws called chelicerae, tipped with sharp fangs ready to inject a lethal venom into its insect prey.

Body segments
The wasp's body has three parts: a head, thorax, and abdomen. The head contains the brain and sense organs. The thorax is packed with wing muscles, and the abdomen contains the heart and intestines.

A network of fine tubes called veins stiffens the wings so they can flex in flight without collapsing.

Most adult insects have wings made of thin plates of chitin – the substance that forms the skeleton.

The crop stores food that the wasp has swallowed but not fully digested.

The heart is an open-ended tube that pumps fluid forward.

Malpighian tubules gather waste and excess water from the blood (called haemolymph), and eject them from the body.

Venom gland

A network of nerve fibres carries nerve signals to and from the brain, and controls movement.

The midgut is where most digestion takes place, and where nutrients are absorbed.

Stinger

Venom sac linked to the wasp's sting stores poison made by the venom gland.

ABDOMEN

'Arthropods are the most successful animals on the planet.'

EXOSKELETON

A bug's exoskeleton is external, with the fleshy tissue inside. It is made of a fingernail-like material called chitin, and has movable joints made of flexible chitin. The skeleton is waterproof, helping to stop body moisture escaping. This allows many insects and spiders to thrive in deserts, where soft-bodied invertebrates such as slugs cannot survive.

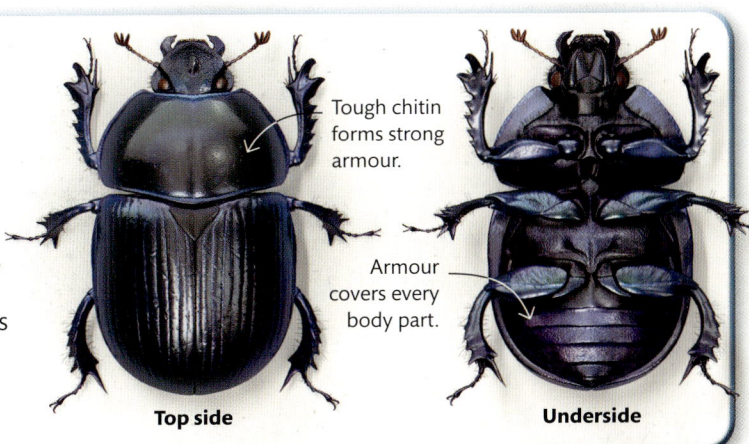

Tough chitin forms strong armour.

Top side

Armour covers every body part.

Underside

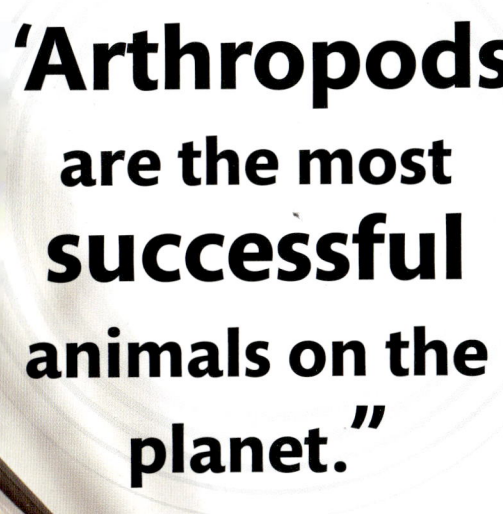

Air sacs

Brain processes information received from the wasp's senses.

Long antennae sense vibrations and detect chemical scent signals.

Complex compound eyes give the wasp the vision it needs to fly and hunt prey.

Salivary gland

Powerful muscles inside the thorax are the driving force for the wasp's wings.

Biting jaws pinch together to cut and chew the wasp's food.

Each leg is a series of stiff tubes, hinged together with flexible joints and worked by internal muscles.

Feet have sharp claws for clinging to surfaces and prey. Some insects such as blow flies also have sticky foot pads.

THORAX

HEAD

TRUE BUGS

The word "bug" is used to describe all kinds of small scuttling or flying creatures such as flies, beetles, and spiders. But to a scientist, a bug is a specific insect group that eats liquid food using a long, tubular beak. These harlequin bugs drink sugary plant sap, but many true bugs suck the juices of other animals, including human blood.

TYPES OF BUGS

There are many types of arthropods – the animals that we often call bugs. They all have the same basic hard-skinned, jointed body structure, but different numbers of body segments and legs. Most of them are either multi-legged myriapods, eight-legged arachnids, or six-legged insects.

"Eighty per cent of all known animal species are arthropods."

CRUSTACEANS

Most crustaceans are oceanic animals, such as crabs and lobsters. There are several types of crab that spend most of their lives on land, but one group - the woodlice - lives here permanently, seeking out damp places. Crustaceans have varying numbers of legs, and some woodlice resemble small millipedes.

WOODLOUSE

ABOUT
67,000
KNOWN SPECIES

ABOUT
13,000
KNOWN SPECIES

MYRIAPODS

These are the centipedes and millipedes with bodies made up of chains of identical segments. A centipede has one pair of legs per segment, while a millipede has two. Centipedes are fast-moving hunters, armed with venomous fangs. Millipedes eat plants, and creep along more slowly.

LONG-JAWED ORB WEAVER SPIDER

SPIDERS

Spiders are arachnids – eight-legged arthropods without wings. These predators prey on insects and other spiders, often trapping them in snares made of silk. Their bodies have only two sections, and they have venomous fangs for killing their prey. A few spiders have a dangerous bite for humans.

BURMESE MILLIPEDE

ABOUT
46,000
KNOWN SPECIES

ABOUT 1,750

KNOWN SPECIES

SCORPIONS

Although scorpions are arachnids like spiders, they have a very different body shape, which is more like a lobster, complete with stout pincers for seizing prey. Their unique feature is a sting on the end of a flexible tail, used for defence or to kill prey. Some scorpions are seriously venomous.

VINEGAROON

RED CLAW SCORPION

OTHER ARACHNIDS

As well as spiders and scorpions, the arachnids also include sun spiders, harvestmen, whip scorpions, and little mites and ticks. The big, dangerous-looking whip scorpions and sun spiders are in fact harmless, whereas tiny ticks are bloodsuckers, and a few can transmit deadly diseases.

ABOUT 96,000

KNOWN SPECIES

INSECTS

All other arthropods are greatly outnumbered by the insects, which make up more than half of the known species on Earth. Their variety is amazing, but all adult insects have six legs, and most have wings. Some sting or bite, and a few carry disease, but many more are breathtakingly beautiful.

GOLDEN JEWEL BEETLE

ABOUT 900,000

KNOWN SPECIES

"Scientists think there may be more than 10 million unknown species of insect."

ON THE MOVE

Most bugs are well equipped for walking, having at least six legs. But the young forms of flies and some other insects have no legs at all, and must wriggle along like worms. Many can swim in ponds and streams, while some spiders and insects can walk on water. Insects such as grasshoppers and fleas are excellent jumpers. Most spectacularly, insects were the first animals on Earth to master flight, and some species are incredibly fast and agile in the air.

Up and away

The cockchafer is a stocky, armoured beetle that does not appear well adapted for flight. But, on the contrary, its tough wing cases (elytra) conceal a pair of long wings that allow this insect to fly off in search of a mate.

The outspread, rigid wing cases act like aircraft wings, providing extra lift.

Strong struts support the wings, but allow them to flex to generate the thrust needed for flight.

This beetle has a hinge in each wing, allowing it to fold them away under the elytra when it lands.

The transparent wing membrane is a thin but complex structure with two layers of tough chitin.

This beetle is just about to land. When it is flying at full speed the legs are tucked in for better streamlining.

TAKING FLIGHT

Most flying insects have two pairs of wings that are linked together, but beetles use only the back pair for flight. When they are not needed, the delicate wings are folded away beneath modified forewings that form protective elytra. This lets the beetle burrow and push through plant stems without risking wing damage. It takes only a second for the wings to be unfurled for take-off.

Ready. . .
In preparation for flight, this cockchafer beetle opens the hinged elytra covering its wings. In cold weather, some insects vibrate their wing muscles to warm up.

Get set. . .
With its elytra open, the beetle can unfold the long hindwings used for flight. Instinctively, the sensitive antennae are used to check the air currents.

Go!
Pushing off with its legs, the cockchafer springs into the air. The hindwings provide the thrust that drives it forward, but the elytra generate lift as it gathers speed.

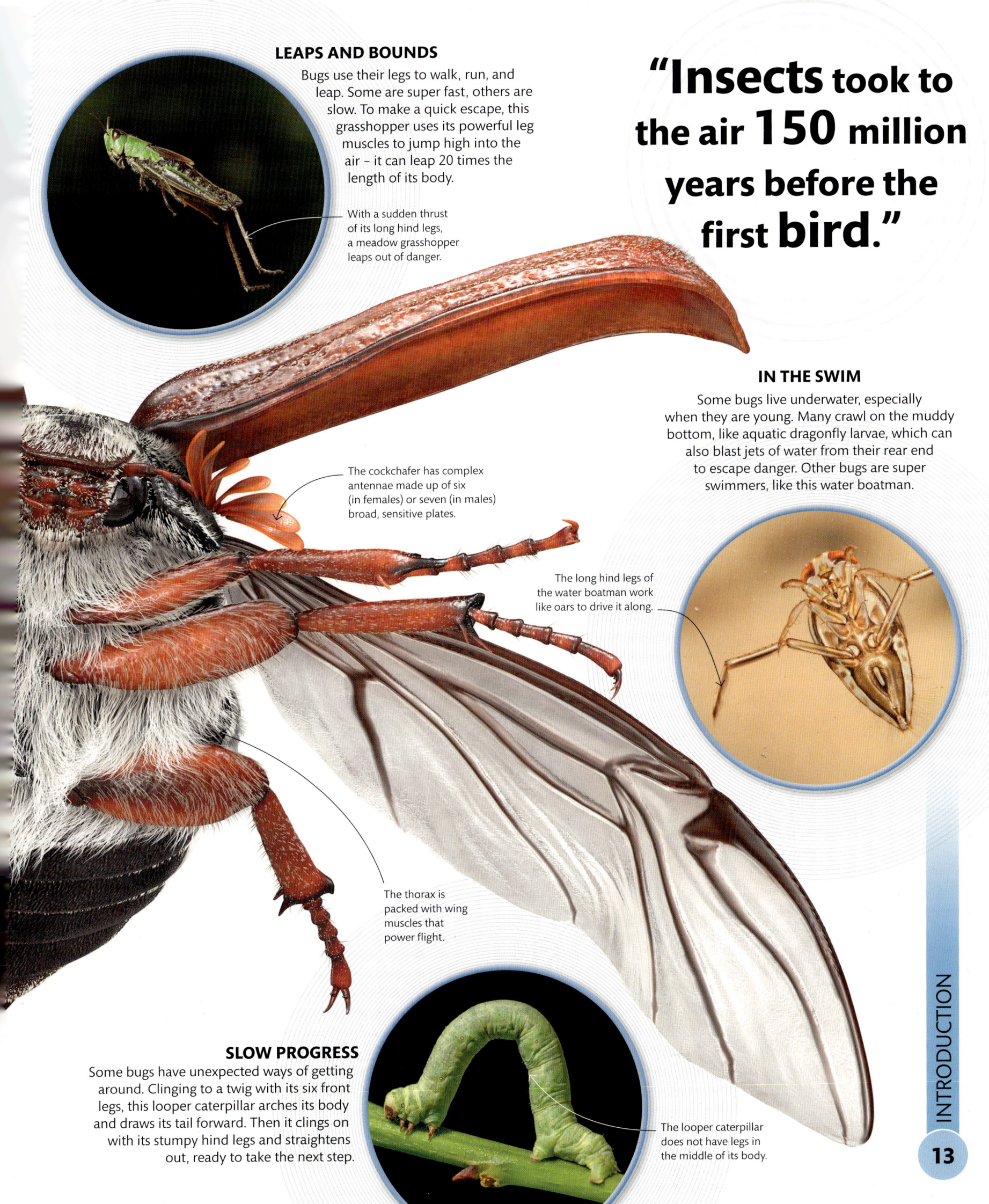

LEAPS AND BOUNDS

Bugs use their legs to walk, run, and leap. Some are super fast, others are slow. To make a quick escape, this grasshopper uses its powerful leg muscles to jump high into the air – it can leap 20 times the length of its body.

With a sudden thrust of its long hind legs, a meadow grasshopper leaps out of danger.

"**Insects** took to the air **150** million years before the first **bird.**"

The cockchafer has complex antennae made up of six (in females) or seven (in males) broad, sensitive plates.

IN THE SWIM

Some bugs live underwater, especially when they are young. Many crawl on the muddy bottom, like aquatic dragonfly larvae, which can also blast jets of water from their rear end to escape danger. Other bugs are super swimmers, like this water boatman.

The long hind legs of the water boatman work like oars to drive it along.

The thorax is packed with wing muscles that power flight.

SLOW PROGRESS

Some bugs have unexpected ways of getting around. Clinging to a twig with its six front legs, this looper caterpillar arches its body and draws its tail forward. Then it clings on with its stumpy hind legs and straightens out, ready to take the next step.

The looper caterpillar does not have legs in the middle of its body.

SKATING HUNTER

Nearly all bugs are small in size. This allows them to get around in ways that would be impossible for bigger, heavier animals. This raft spider hunts by skating over the surface of freshwater pools. It is covered with velvety, water-repelling hairs that allow the surface film to support its weight. It detects prey by sensing ripples in the water, seizes it with its front legs, and kills it with a venomous bite.

GROWING UP

A bug's tough exoskeleton cannot stretch as the animal grows. This forces the bug to break out of the old, hard skin and expand a new, soft skin. The process is difficult and dangerous for many bugs; because they are soft, they are vulnerable to attack. Many species shed their skin under cover of darkness or well away from prying eyes.

TRIALS OF LIFE

Most animals start life as smaller versions of their parents, and gradually get bigger. Many arthropods grow this way. When baby scorpions and spiders hatch, their bodies are almost exactly like their mother's, complete with eight legs. This makes shedding their skins a very difficult operation.

Mother scorpion
Newly hatched baby scorpions are carried on their mother's back to keep them safe from predators.

Each baby scorpion has eight legs, a pair of pincers, and a tiny sting.

HARD TIMES

An arthropod must shed its exoskeleton to get bigger. The old cuticle (skin) separates from the new one and splits open, allowing the animal to extract its body. Then it has to pump up the new, soft cuticle with fluid or air to make the skin bigger before it hardens. The cuticle takes about two hours to harden into a tough exoskeleton, leaving the animal very vulnerable to attack because it has no protection and cannot escape.

Desert locust grows wing buds at the fourth stage of its development.

COMPLETE REBUILD

Butterflies, moths, flies, and many other insects do not start life as nymphs. Instead, they hatch as soft-skinned larvae known as caterpillars or grubs. Their sausage-shaped bodies allow them to shed their skin easily and safely. They spend all their time eating and growing, before their bodies are completely rebuilt as winged adults.

The fully grown monarch caterpillar attaches itself to a twig with silk.

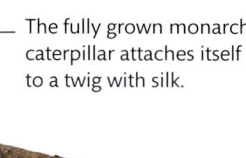

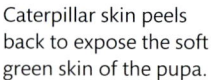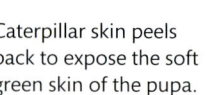

Stage 1: Egg
A butterfly has a four-stage life cycle. It starts life as a tiny egg, which the female butterfly usually lays on a particular type of plant. The American monarch butterfly, shown here, lays her eggs on milkweed plants.

Stage 2: Larva
The egg hatches as a tiny, soft-bodied caterpillar – a butterfly larva. The larva eats its own eggshell before munching milkweed leaves. The more it eats, the bigger it gets, shedding its flexible skin four times before reaching full size.

Stage 3: Pupa
When the caterpillar is fully grown, it stops eating and sheds its skin for a fifth time. The skin peels off to reveal a pupa – the stage of the monarch's life when its body is transformed into a butterfly. This takes about two weeks.

Caterpillar skin peels back to expose the soft green skin of the pupa.

Moulting spider

A spider must replace its exoskeleton many times as it grows. Each time it has to extract every part of this complex body, being careful not to damage the new, soft cuticle or break a leg. This is not easy, and many spiders die in the process, never reaching breeding age.

The soft cuticle of a newly moulted spider cannot support its weight.

Stage by stage

Scorpions and spiders do not change much as they grow. Some insects have similar growth stages, but as they get bigger, they gradually change their form. A locust, for example, slowly develops wings that become fully formed at the final stage.

ALTERNATIVE LIFESTYLES

The early life stages of locusts are called nymphs. Although they look like the adults and live in the same way, they cannot fly. But the nymphs of some insects lead different lives. A dragonfly nymph lives underwater, passing through several growth stages before it climbs out of the water and sheds its cuticle for the last time, as seen here, to become an adult.

Pupa gets shorter, and the protective skin becomes smoother and harder.

Pupa splits, and the new butterfly starts pushing its way out.

Developing wings are visible through the skin of the pupa.

Stage 4: Adult

When the adult butterfly is fully formed inside the pupa, the outer skin splits open. The butterfly hauls itself out, and pumps up its wings to full size before they harden. This is the final life stage; the butterfly never sheds its skin again.

At first the body looks too fat compared to the wings, but it soon starts changing shape.

Fluid pumped into the wings makes them expand, and the transformation is complete.

AMAZING ANATOMY

Bugs may be small, but look closer and you will discover just how amazing they are. Their bodies often take astonishing forms, with extraordinary adaptations for survival. While some species go unnoticed thanks to clever camouflage, others stand out from the crowd by glittering like living jewels.

FIREPOWER
AFRICAN BOMBARDIER BEETLE

The African bombardier beetle looks harmless, but it has a secret weapon. This beetle is armed with its own chemical gun, which makes a searingly hot, toxic spray blast from its tail end to scald and blister any animal that attacks it. The beetle can aim the spray with incredible precision to inflict maximum damage on its enemy.

CHEMICAL WEAPON

When the bombardier beetle is alarmed, chemicals stored in two elastic sacs inside its tail end are squirted into a pair of armoured chambers. Here they mix with a substance called an enzyme that triggers a chemical reaction, blasting the hot mixture out of a movable nozzle with a "pop" sound.

As with all beetles, the front wings are a pair of protective wing cases called elytra.

Chemicals are stored safely in a muscular sac.

Sac squeezes the chemicals through a valve into the reaction chamber.

Gland produces the chemicals.

Spray is fired from the flexible ejection nozzle.

Chamber wall releases enzymes that make the chemicals explode.

Two sacs store the chemicals – hydroquinone and hydrogen peroxide.

Reaction chambers are made of tough chitin – the same material as the insect's hard exoskeleton.

STATS AND FACTS

ABOUT

500
SPECIES

Found in most parts of the world, bombardier beetles have developed one of the most explosive defence mechanisms in the animal world.

TEMPERATURE OF SPRAY
100°C (212°F) maximum

SPEED OF SPRAY
2.5–20 m/sec (8–65 ft/sec)

SPRAYING DISTANCE

Up to 30 cm for a 2 cm-long beetle

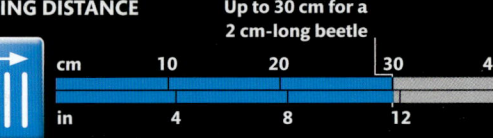

cm		10	20		30	40
in		4	8		12	

ADULT LIFESPAN

5-6 WEEKS

Blistering beetles

Many species of small beetle living all over the world have evolved this type of chemical defence. But unlike some, the African bombardier beetle is able to aim its toxic spray accurately in almost any direction.

The beetle uses its long, sensitive antennae to detect the movement or scent of prey and predators.

Like nearly all adult insects, a bombardier beetle has compound eyes with hundreds of lenses.

Biting mouthparts are adapted for eating other insects.

HOT SHOT

An African bombardier beetle can rotate the nozzle at the tip of its abdomen to blast its defensive spray directly at an attacker. Tiny shield-like deflectors fine-tune its aim, so it can fire over its back or between its legs, as well as straight backwards. The hot chemical mixture is strong enough to paralyse an attacking ant or spider.

Ants are dangerous foes, with powerful bites and stings, but the bombardier's chemical spray can drive them away.

Pulses of spray are fired in rapid succession.

Long legs allow the beetle to run fast for its size – but many of its enemies can run faster.

"The spray is blasted out at 500 pulses per second."

AT A GLANCE

- **SIZE** 2 cm (¾ in) long

- **HABITAT** Woodlands and grasslands

- **LOCATION** Africa south of the Sahara

- **DIET** Other insects and similar animals such as spiders

AMAZING ANATOMY

MOST LEGS

SPIRAL DEFENCE
If it senses danger, a millipede
quickly coils up in a tight
spiral – its tough body armour
protects the soft underside.
The vivid colours of this tropical
millipede warn birds that its
body oozes foul-smelling oils.

LEG POWER
FIRE MILLIPEDE

Millipedes have more legs than any other animal on the planet. Some have more than 700, but no millipede has a thousand legs – the meaning of the word "millipede". Their long bodies are divided into many circular armoured segments, and each segment carries two pairs of legs. This big fire millipede lives in the tropical forests of Madagascar. Like most millipedes, it eats mainly dead, rotting plants – it is far too slow-moving to catch other animals, despite having all those legs.

AT A GLANCE

- **SIZE** Up to 18 cm (7 in) long, with up to 63 body segments
- **HABITAT** Tropical forest floor and on low-growing plants
- **LOCATION** Madagascar
- **DIET** Decaying vegetable matter, such as leaves

STATS AND FACTS

ABOUT
12,000
SPECIES

Millipedes are found throughout the world. They are slow movers but powerful burrowers – some can push easily through the hardest, driest soil.

ADULT LIFESPAN
10 YEARS

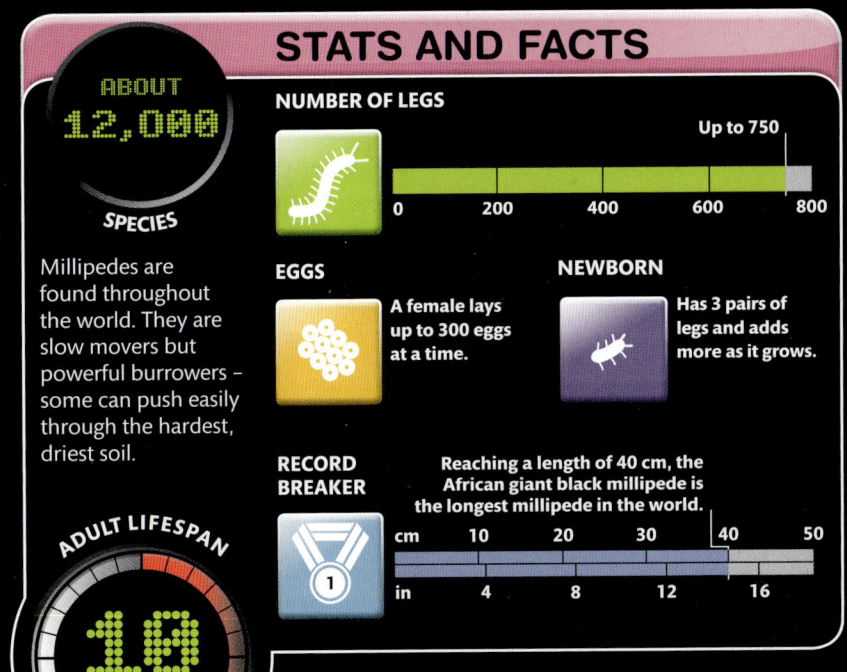

NUMBER OF LEGS

0	200	400	600	800

Up to 750

EGGS
A female lays up to 300 eggs at a time.

NEWBORN
Has 3 pairs of legs and adds more as it grows.

RECORD BREAKER
Reaching a length of 40 cm, the African giant black millipede is the longest millipede in the world.

cm	10	20	30	40	50
in	4	8	12	16	

BIGGEST SPIDER

HAIRY DEFENCE

Like all tarantulas, the Goliath spider has fangs that stab downwards instead of pinching together like those of typical spiders. To humans, its venom is no worse than a wasp sting. In self-defence, the spider may also rub its body to release a cloud of tiny irritating hairs.

GIANT-SIZED
GOLIATH SPIDER

With stout hairy legs that could span a page of this book, the Goliath spider is the biggest spider on Earth. A massively built tarantula, it prowls the forest floor at night-time in search of large insects, lizards, and even the occasional snake. Although it can use its huge, hollow fangs to inject prey with a paralysing dose of venom, the Goliath spider often relies on sheer muscle power to overwhelm and kill its victims. By day, it retreats to a burrow to stay safe from enemies.

AT A GLANCE

- **SIZE** Body 12–14 cm (4¾–5½ in) long
- **HABITAT** Tropical rainforest
- **LOCATION** South America
- **DIET** Worms, insects, frogs, small reptiles, and rodents

STATS AND FACTS

ABOUT
900
SPECIES

The tarantulas are heavyweight hunters that live in tropical or subtropical regions. There is also a European tarantula, but it belongs to a different spider family.

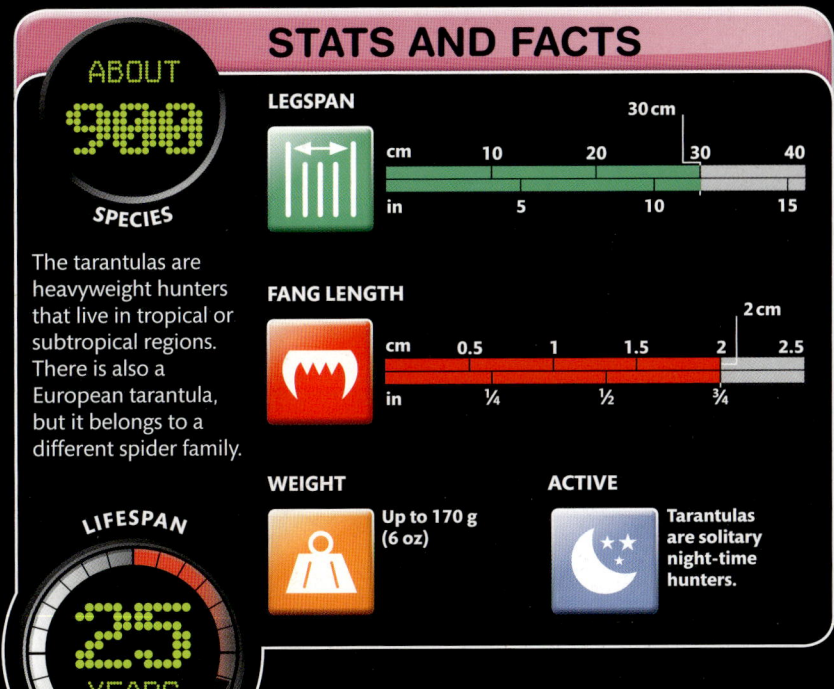

LEGSPAN

cm	10	20	30 cm / 30	40
in	5	10		15

FANG LENGTH

cm	0.5	1	1.5	2 / 2 cm	2.5
in	¼	½	¾		

WEIGHT
Up to 170 g (6 oz)

ACTIVE
Tarantulas are solitary night-time hunters.

LIFESPAN
25
YEARS

OUT OF THE BLUE
MORPHO BUTTERFLY

The shimmering, iridescent blue of the tropical morpho butterfly is one of nature's most dazzling sights. It is the effect of sunlight reflected by the wings, creating their electric blue colour. As the butterfly beats its wings the colour flashes on and off.

Winged wonder
Many butterflies have vibrant colours, but few have the striking visual impact of tropical morphos. Males are a more vivid blue than the females, which shows most clearly during their territorial wing-flashing display flights.

> "Blue morphos are some of the **largest** butterflies in the world."

SMALL SCALES
The wings of most butterflies are covered in tiny scales. They are layered like roof tiles, as seen in this image of a morpho wing. The scales have microscopic ridges that scatter reflected light to create the iridescent metallic blue effect.

STATS AND FACTS

29 SPECIES

Many species of morpho butterflies live in the tropical forests of Central and South America, but they are not all bright blue.

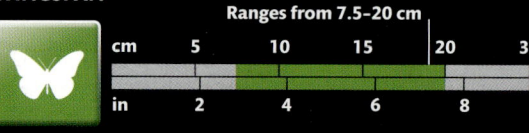

WINGSPAN

Ranges from 7.5–20 cm

cm	5	10	15	20	30
in	2	4	6	8	

DEFENCE

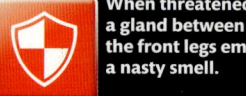

When threatened, a gland between the front legs emits a nasty smell.

STATUS

!

Morpho butterflies are severely affected by habitat loss and over-collection.

ADULT LIFESPAN

2–3 WEEKS

Big eyespots help to deter predators.

When the morpho butterfly perches in the shade, the wings are usually kept closed to hide the bright blue colour.

SHADY SECRET

By contrast, the blue morpho's underwings are dull brown with eye spots. They provide excellent camouflage in the dappled light of the tropical forest, hiding the morpho from predatory birds and other enemies.

Long antennae detect airborne food smells, such as ripe fruit.

Compound eyes

AT A GLANCE

- **SIZE** Wingspan up to 15 cm (6 in)
- **HABITAT** Tropical rainforests
- **LOCATION** Central America and northern South America
- **DIET** Adults sip the juice of rotting fruit, as well as fluids from dead animals and animal waste; caterpillars eat leaves

The spectacular iridescent wings are edged in black.

CATERPILLAR WARS

Morpho caterpillars bristle with fine hairs that irritate the skin, providing protection against potential enemies. They eat the leaves of plants belonging to the pea family. If too many caterpillars are trying to feed on the same plant, they are very likely to attack and eat each other.

AMAZING ANATOMY

TAKING COVER

Some harvestmen live in groups, which is safer than living alone. This group in the tropical forest of Costa Rica is using a leaf to shelter from the rain, for each raindrop is as big as a harvestman's body.

ALL LEGS
HARVESTMAN

It looks like a very leggy spider, but a harvestman is a different sort of animal. Although it is related to spiders and has eight long legs, it has a bean-shaped body with just two eyes perched on top. It gathers food with a pair of strong jaws called chelicerae. They are like the jaws of spiders, but instead of carrying venomous fangs, they end in a pair of pincers used for tearing food apart before swallowing the tiny pieces. A harvestman finds its food mainly by scent and touch, feeling its way with its extra-long second pair of legs.

AT A GLANCE

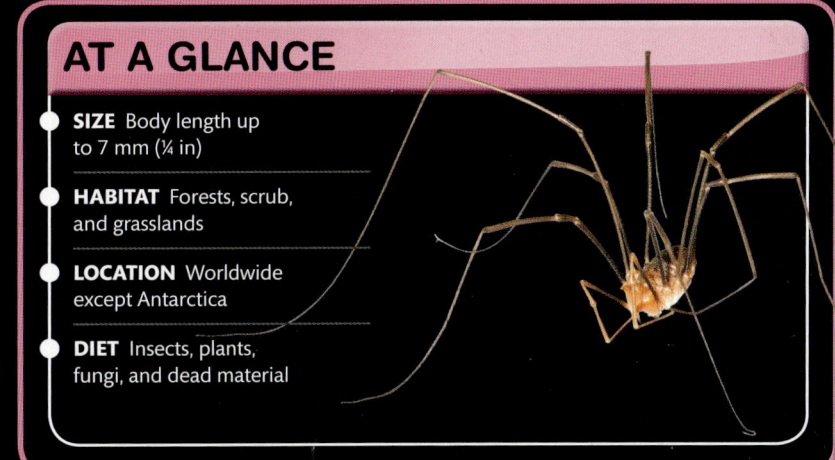

- **SIZE** Body length up to 7 mm (¼ in)
- **HABITAT** Forests, scrub, and grasslands
- **LOCATION** Worldwide except Antarctica
- **DIET** Insects, plants, fungi, and dead material

STATS AND FACTS

ABOUT 6,500 SPECIES

Harvestmen walk on raised legs and so look as if they are walking on stilts. They often clean their legs by pulling them through their jaws.

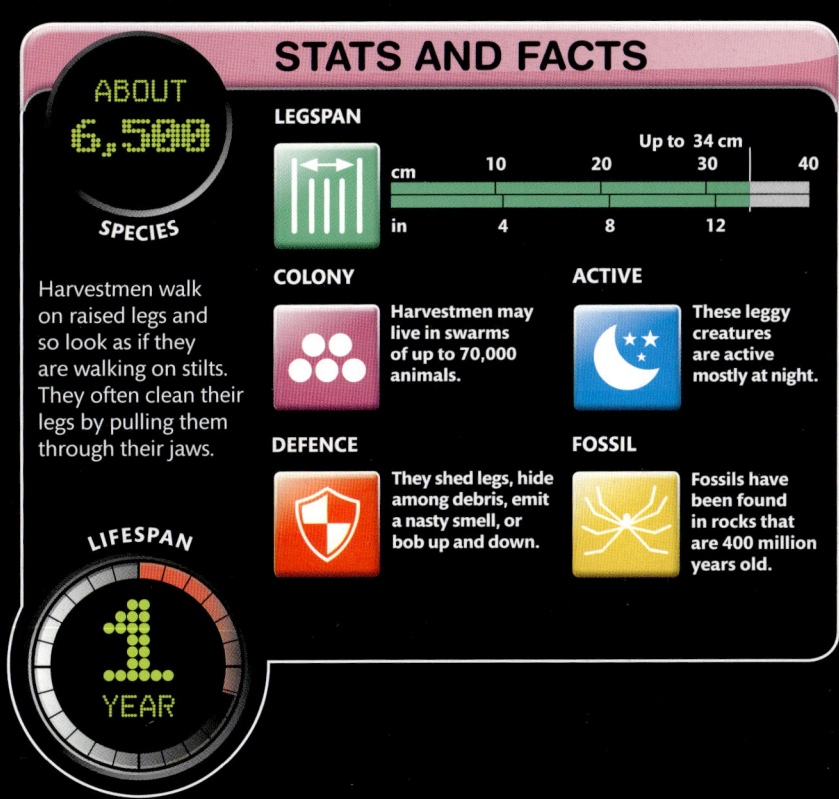

LEGSPAN

| cm | | 10 | 20 | Up to 34 cm 30 | 40 |
| in | | 4 | 8 | 12 | |

COLONY Harvestmen may live in swarms of up to 70,000 animals.

ACTIVE These leggy creatures are active mostly at night.

DEFENCE They shed legs, hide among debris, emit a nasty smell, or bob up and down.

FOSSIL Fossils have been found in rocks that are 400 million years old.

LIFESPAN
1 YEAR

MONSTER BUG
GIANT WETA

New Zealand is the home of some of the world's biggest insects – the giant wetas. The largest of these flightless crickets can grow to the size of a mouse. It is so big and heavy that it cannot leap away from danger, and relies on scaring away its enemies by hissing at them like a snake. It had few enemies until Europeans colonized New Zealand and introduced cats, rats, and other hunters. These have made many giant wetas rare, and the biggest one now lives only on Little Barrier Island off the northern coast.

AT A GLANCE

- **SIZE** Body up to 10 cm (4 in) long
- **HABITAT** Forest, usually in the trees
- **LOCATION** New Zealand
- **DIET** Leaves, mosses, flowers, and fruit

STATS AND FACTS

ABOUT 11 SPECIES OF GIANT WETA

The word weta comes from the local language of New Zealand, Maori. A giant weta is called *wetapunga*, which means "the god of ugly things".

GROWTH

Length when newly hatched is 0.5 cm

cm	2	4	6	8	10
in	1	2	3	

Length of an adult is 7–10 cm

WEIGHT

Wetas can weigh up to 71 g (2½ oz).

EGGS

The female lays up to 300 eggs in her lifetime.

MOULT

The growing young shed their thick outer casing 10 times.

STATUS

Wetas are endangered due to habitat loss and predators.

LIFESPAN

2 YEARS

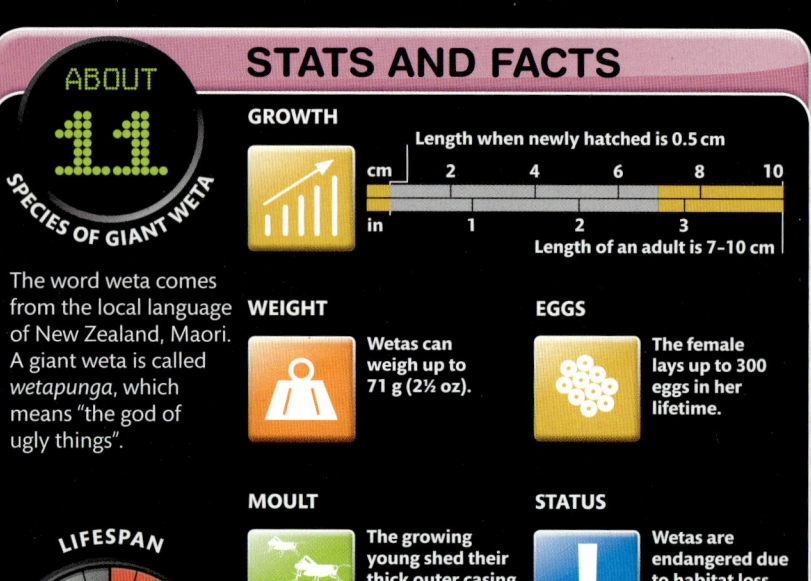

BITING JAWS

There are at least 70 different species of weta, including 11 giant wetas – all found only in New Zealand. Most of the smaller species prey on other insects, but the giant wetas eat leaves and moss. They have strong jaws and a powerful bite, but are shy and secretive and only come out to feed at night.

SUPER-SIZED BUTTERFLY

QUEEN ALEXANDRA'S BIRDWING

This spectacular tropical butterfly has a wingspan bigger than that of many birds. It flies high into the treetops, where it sips nectar from the flowers of climbing vines. The female butterfly lays her eggs on the same vines, which contain weak poisons. When the caterpillars hatch they eat the vines, building up the poisons in their bodies. This makes them taste horrible, protecting them from predators.

AT A GLANCE

- **SIZE** Body length up to 8 cm (3 in); wingspan up to 28 cm (11 in)
- **HABITAT** Lowland tropical rainforest
- **LOCATION** Eastern Papua New Guinea
- **DIET** Caterpillar eats foliage of Aristolochia vines; adult sips nectar from flowers, usually of same plant

STATS AND FACTS

ABOUT 36 BIRDWING SPECIES

Birdwing butterflies live only in the Far East, from India to northern Australia.

STATUS Three species are endangered due to habitat loss and poaching.

EGGS Up to 240 eggs are laid during the 3-month lifespan.

FLIGHT SPEED Up to 15 km/h

km/h	5	10	15	20
mph	5		10	

ADULT LIFESPAN 3 MONTHS

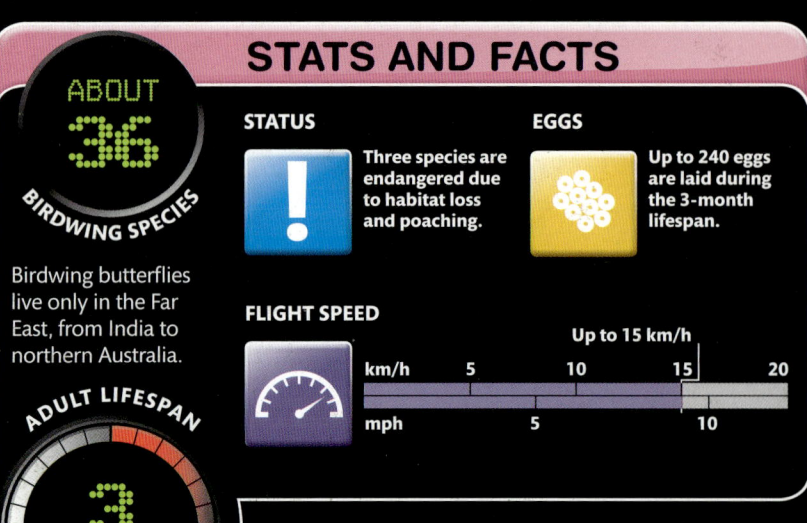

BIGGEST BUTTERFLY

GLITTERING MALE

The dazzling male butterfly is far more vividly coloured than the female, which is bigger but mainly brown with white wing markings. Males court females by hovering above them on their long, iridescent wings, releasing a sweet-smelling fragrance.

"This birdwing is one of the **rarest** butterflies in the world."

UNSINKABLE BUG
POND SKATER

This slender bug is so light that it can walk on water. The strong bonds that hold water molecules together form an elastic surface film, strong enough for the pond skater to stand on. But the surface film can also trap other insects, making them easy prey for the pond skater, which darts rapidly across the water to attack them.

Specialized legs

A pond skater looks as if it has only two pairs of legs, but there is a third, shorter pair at the front used for catching prey. The bug skates across the water with its long middle pair of legs, steering with the back pair.

HAIRY LEGS

The pond skater's legs are covered with velvety hairs. The hairs trap tiny air bubbles that stop its feet from getting wet and sticking to the surface film. Instead, they simply flex the water surface, as if the bug was standing on a trampoline. Similar hairs covering the rest of the pond skater's body ensure that it never sinks.

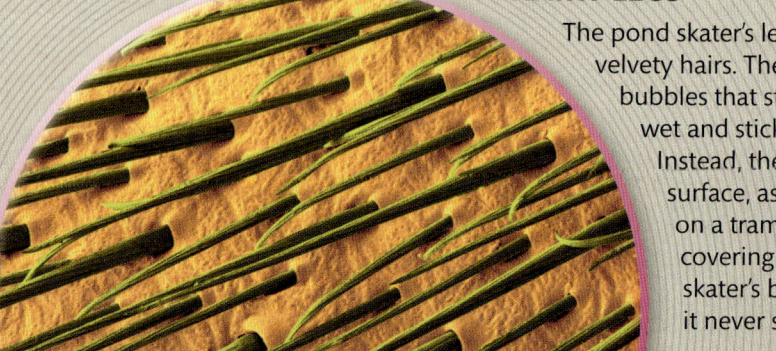

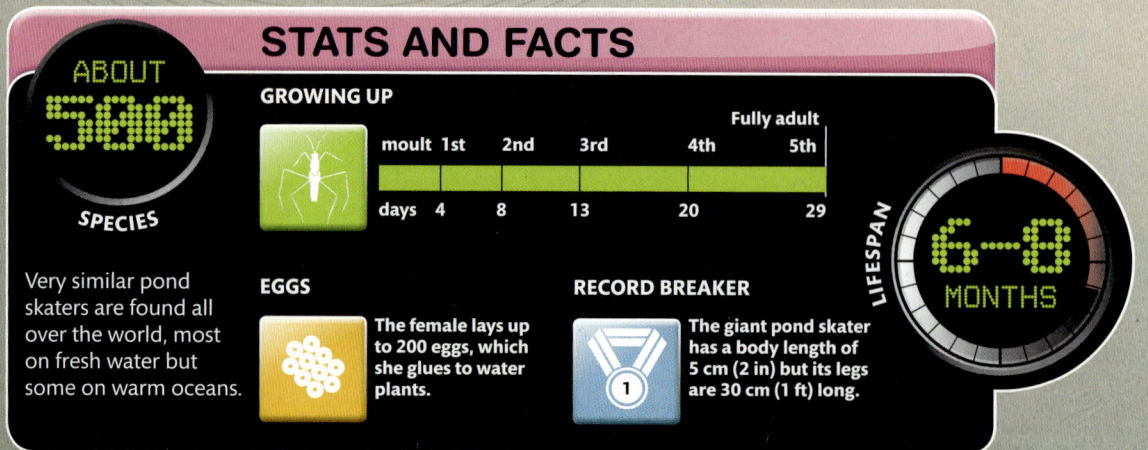

The skater uses its middle pair of legs like oars to propel itself over the water.

The skater's legs detect ripples on the water, which betray struggling prey.

STATS AND FACTS

ABOUT 500 SPECIES

Very similar pond skaters are found all over the world, most on fresh water but some on warm oceans.

GROWING UP

	moult	1st	2nd	3rd	4th	Fully adult 5th
days	4	8	13	20	29	

EGGS

The female lays up to 200 eggs, which she glues to water plants.

RECORD BREAKER

The giant pond skater has a body length of 5 cm (2 in) but its legs are 30 cm (1 ft) long.

LIFESPAN 6-8 MONTHS

"Pond skaters move at 1.5 m (5 ft) per second – as quick as the blink of an eye."

The light, slender body is covered with hairs that prevent it from sinking.

AT A GLANCE

- **Size** About 1 cm (¼ in)
- **Habitat** Ponds, lakes, streams, and rivers
- **Location** Europe
- **Diet** Small animals on the water surface

WALKS ON WATER

Short, strong front legs are used for seizing prey.

An ant trapped by the surface film of the water makes easy prey.

TOXIC BEAK

Like all true bugs, the pond skater does not have jaws. Instead, it has a sharp stabbing beak that injects a dose of toxic saliva into prey. The fluid digests the soft tissues inside the victim's hard exoskeleton, turning them into a liquid that the pond skater sucks up.

AMAZING ANATOMY

35

BRIGHTEST BUG
FIREFLY

Few bugs are as astonishing as the fireflies. These flying beetles shine in the night sky, thanks to special light organs in the tail ends of their bodies that attract breeding partners. A chemical reaction creates the light without generating any heat, and the firefly can turn the light on and off when it likes. While many fireflies glow in the dark, others flash with distinctive patterns.

Long antennae are sensitive to touch, taste, and scent.

Big eyes help the firefly pick out the signals of others.

FLASH PATTERNS

In North America, there are many closely related species of fireflies. Each one flashes with its own distinctive pattern as it flies, allowing the fireflies to recognize each other. Some use sequences of short flashes with long and short gaps between them, while others flash for longer to create glowing shapes on summer nights.

Photinus umbratus

Photinus marginellus

Photinus consimilis

Photinus collustrans

Fatal attraction

This American *Photuris* firefly uses its light organs to flash signals to other fireflies. When the female sees the flash code of a male, she flashes an invitation back to mate. But she can also mimic the signal of a female *Photinus* firefly to attract a *Photinus* male – and when he lands, she eats him.

SNAIL PREY

The larvae of many fireflies are fierce predators that eat snails. The hungry larva seizes a snail with a pair of sharp jaws that inject digestive juices. These turn the snail's tissues to soup, ready for the larva to drink. This is the larva of a European glowworm – a type of firefly.

STATS AND FACTS

ABOUT 2,000 SPECIES

Fireflies live all over the world. The females of some species cannot fly, and are known as glowworms.

EFFICIENCY

Ninety-eight per cent of the energy used by the firefly's light organ is turned into light.

LIFE CYCLE

Larva lives for a year, pupates for two weeks, then lives as an adult.

DEFENCE

A firefly's body contains toxins that make it taste unpleasant.

LIGHT

The light produced by fireflies can be yellow, orange, or green.

ADULT LIFESPAN

8 WEEKS

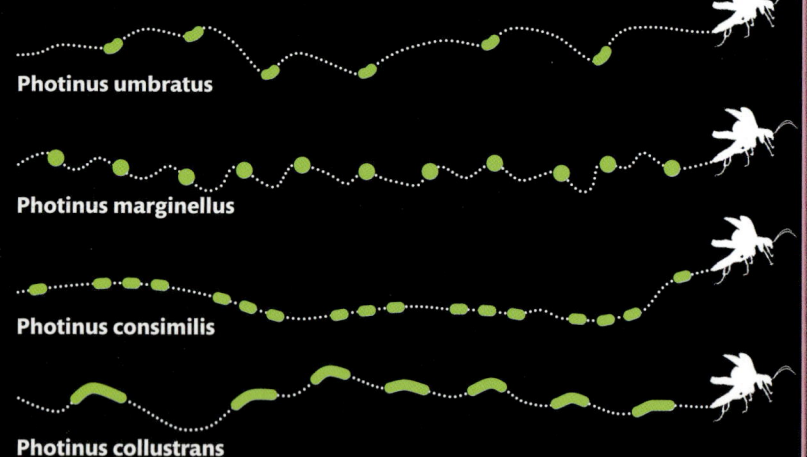

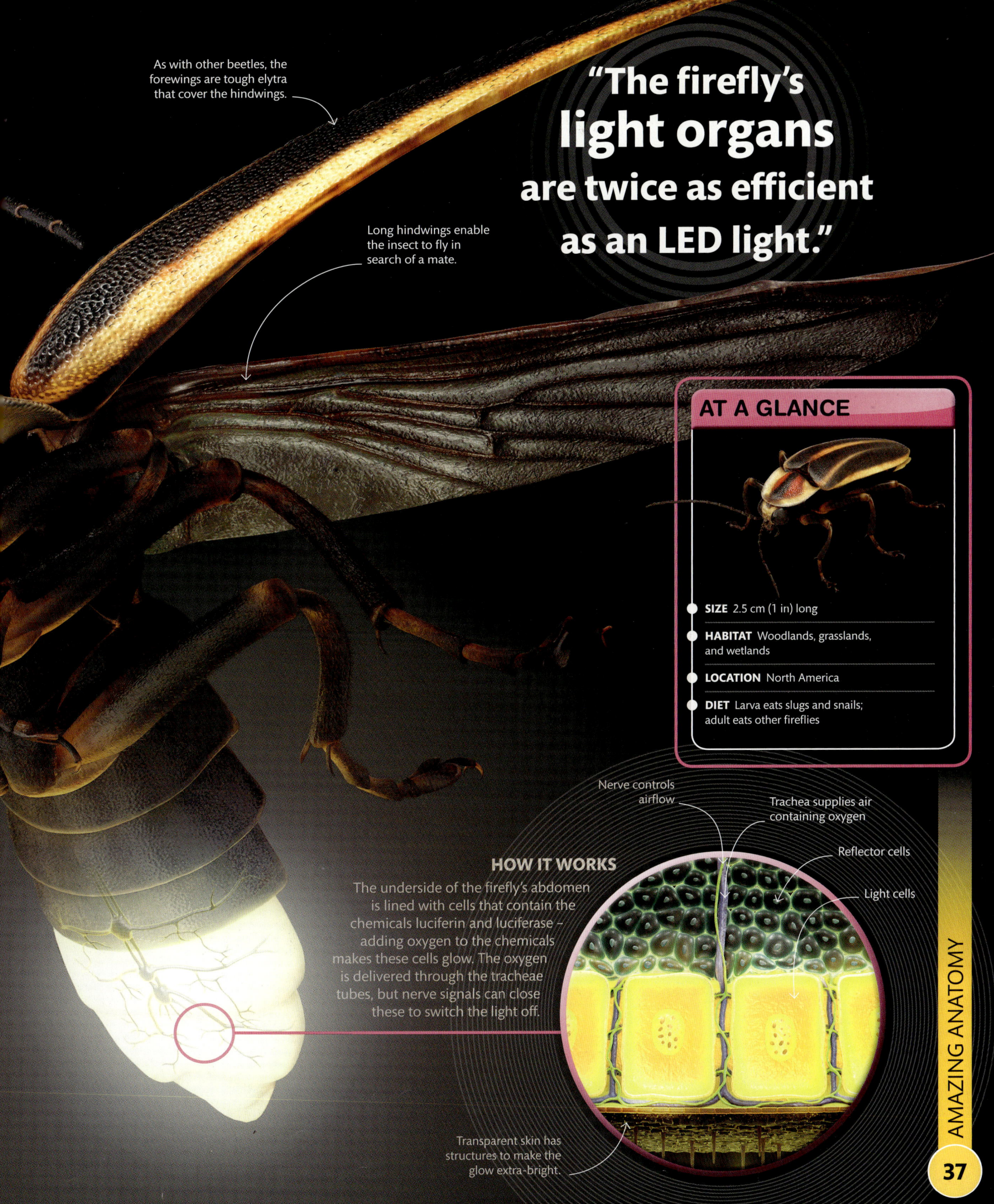

As with other beetles, the forewings are tough elytra that cover the hindwings.

Long hindwings enable the insect to fly in search of a mate.

"The firefly's light organs are twice as efficient as an LED light."

AT A GLANCE

SIZE 2.5 cm (1 in) long

HABITAT Woodlands, grasslands, and wetlands

LOCATION North America

DIET Larva eats slugs and snails; adult eats other fireflies

Nerve controls airflow

Trachea supplies air containing oxygen

Reflector cells

Light cells

HOW IT WORKS

The underside of the firefly's abdomen is lined with cells that contain the chemicals luciferin and luciferase – adding oxygen to the chemicals makes these cells glow. The oxygen is delivered through the tracheae tubes, but nerve signals can close these to switch the light off.

Transparent skin has structures to make the glow extra-bright.

AMAZING ANATOMY

37

LIGHTNING BUGS

Some fireflies found in warmer parts of the world, such as Southeast Asia, live in loose colonies that all flash at once, like flickering lightning. This synchronized light show can make a whole tree glitter with thousands of yellow-green lights, then go dark. Scientists still do not know why these fireflies flash together in such spectacular style.

LEAF MIMIC

The leaves on this tropical tree may look normal, but look again. There are three leaf insects clinging to the twigs in full view. To complete their disguise, the insects even sway slowly in the breeze, just like real leaves.

MASTER OF DISGUISE
MALAYSIAN LEAF INSECT

The leaf insects have evolved the most spectacular camouflage in the animal kingdom. They are relatives of stick insects, but with flattened green or brown bodies that look almost exactly like leaves – with leaf midribs, veins, and even dark marks that mimic leaf damage. Their legs have broad plates and these look like the remains of leaves that have been nibbled by other insects. This astonishing disguise helps protect them from birds, which hunt by sight among the trees for insect prey and do not notice the leaf insects hanging among the foliage.

AT A GLANCE

- **SIZE** 5–10 cm (2–4 in)
- **HABITAT** Tropical forests
- **LOCATION** Malaysia
- **DIET** Leaves

STATS AND FACTS

ABOUT
54
SPECIES

Leaf insects are found from South Asia through to Australia.

ADULT LIFESPAN
7
MONTHS

EGGS
A female can lay up to 500 eggs during her lifetime.

ACTIVE
Leaf insects often feed at night, making them harder to spot.

COLOUR-CHANGING
Young leaf insects are dark red at first.

Adult colours vary from green to brownish yellow.

TREETOP CAMOUFLAGE
GIANT STICK INSECT

A tropical giant stick insect can grow to more than half a metre (20 inches) in length – that's as long as your arm from wrist to shoulder. It is the longest insect on Earth. As with all stick insects, its super-slimline body shape is a form of camouflage, enabling the insect to hide by resembling the twigs of the trees it lives on. Stick insects rarely move during the day, except to complete their disguise by swaying in the wind, in rhythm with the forest foliage around them. The species shown here is the Titan stick insect – one of the longest insects in Australia.

AT A GLANCE

- **SIZE** Body length up to 27 cm (10½ in); with its legs extended 34 cm (13¼ in)
- **HABITAT** Woodlands
- **LOCATION** Northeastern Australia
- **DIET** Leaves of trees such as cypress, acacia, and eucalyptus as well as some other plants

STATS AND FACTS

ABOUT 2,400 SPECIES

Stick insects are found in the warmer regions of the world.

ADULT LIFESPAN 3 YEARS

RECORD BREAKERS

The smallest stick insect measures about 1.1 cm.

cm	10	20	30	40	50	60
in	4	8	12	16	20	

The longest stick insect measures 56 cm (with front legs extended).

DEFENCE Some species feign death, shed a limb, emit a nasty smell, or lash out.

EGGS Some stick insects can lay up to 2,000 eggs.

LONGEST INSECT

LEAF LOCATOR

As night falls, the Titan stick insect leaves its daytime perch and climbs slowly through the trees in search of food. It rarely has to look far, because it eats leaves, chewing them to a pulp with tough, sharp jaws.

SPECIAL ROLE

Like all ants, honeypot ants live in colonies controlled by a single breeding queen. She is looked after by worker ants, which build the nest and gather food. These food-storing ants are specialized workers.

LIVING FOOD RESERVES
HONEYPOT ANTS

These Australian ants are so swollen with food that they can only cling to the roof of their underground nest. But they have not simply over-eaten. They are used as living food stores by the other ants in the nest, which feed them nectar, animal juices, and even water until their bodies inflate like balloons. They may stay like this for many months, ready for when food and water are scarce. Then the other ants come and drain the sugary liquid from their bodies, ensuring that the colony survives until food is easy to find again.

AT A GLANCE

- **SIZE** Worker ant 6 mm (¼ in) long
- **HABITAT** Tropical grasslands and deserts
- **LOCATION** Australia
- **DIET** Flower nectar, fruit, and other insects

STATS AND FACTS

ABOUT 34 SPECIES

All honeypot ants live in places such as deserts, where food is often hard to find.

COLONY

Depending on species, there can be up to 15,000 honeypot ants in a colony.

| | 0 | 5,000 | 10,000 | 15,000 | 20,000 |

EGGS

Honeypot queens can lay up to 1,500 eggs per day.

WEIGHT

Swollen ants are 100 times heavier than other workers.

LIFESPAN OF A COLONY

AVERAGE 10 YEARS

ASTONISHING SENSE OF SMELL

AUTOPILOT
The twin antennae of this male giant emperor moth bristle with chemical sensors. When one antenna detects a stronger fragrance than the other, the moth automatically turns that way to stay on target.

SUPER-SENSITIVE ANTENNAE
GIANT EMPEROR MOTH

The feathery antennae of a male emperor moth are acutely sensitive to a particular type of scent carried on the breeze – the fragrance released by a newly hatched female moth. The male's antennae can detect a tiny quantity of this substance, known as a pheromone, from an astonishing distance. This allows him to track her down and mate with her to produce the next generation of moths. This is an adult emperor moth's only aim in life, for it cannot eat, and lives for barely a month.

AT A GLANCE

- **SIZE** Wingspan up to 15 cm (6 in)
- **HABITAT** Open country with low shrubs
- **LOCATION** Europe and western Asia
- **DIET** Adults do not feed; caterpillars eat leaves of woody plants

STATS AND FACTS

ABOUT 18 SPECIES

As well as as Europe and Asia, emperor moths are also found in North America.

ADULT LIFESPAN

4 WEEKS

EGGS
Female produces up to 100 eggs, laid in clusters of about 20.

GROWTH
Eggs take 10–30 days to hatch.

SCENT

The scent can be detected from 10 km (6 miles) away.

DEFENCE

Big eyespots on the emperor moth's wings may scare away predators.

BIGGEST BUG
HERCULES BEETLE

The mighty Hercules beetle is one of the biggest insects on Earth, with some males reaching lengths of more than 15 cm (6 in). This is because a male has a huge horn projecting from the front section of his body. He has a similar horn on his head, so when he lifts his head the horns pinch together like a pair of jaws. The beetle uses them to wrestle with rival males.

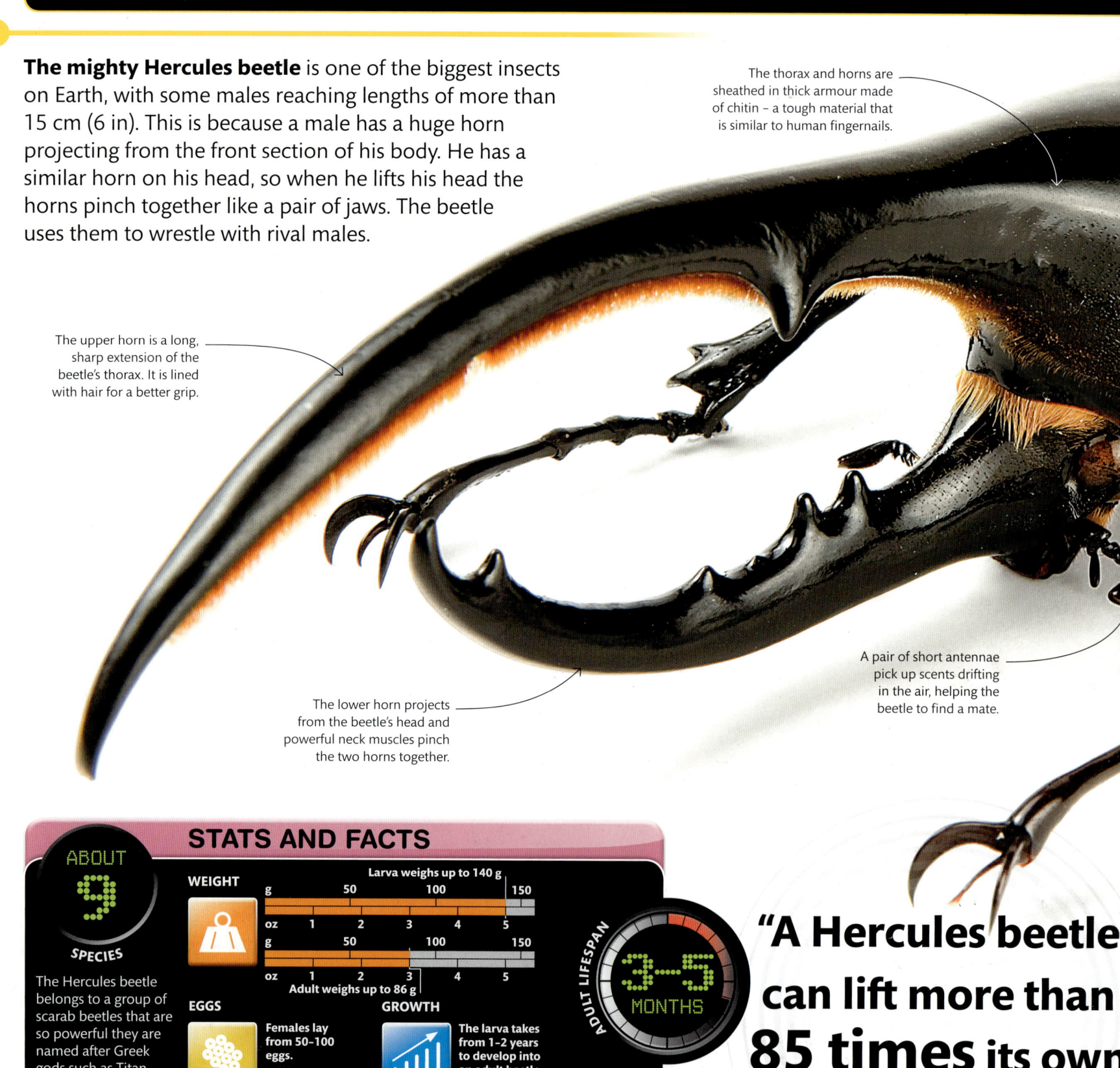

The thorax and horns are sheathed in thick armour made of chitin – a tough material that is similar to human fingernails.

The upper horn is a long, sharp extension of the beetle's thorax. It is lined with hair for a better grip.

The lower horn projects from the beetle's head and powerful neck muscles pinch the two horns together.

A pair of short antennae pick up scents drifting in the air, helping the beetle to find a mate.

STATS AND FACTS

ABOUT 9 SPECIES

The Hercules beetle belongs to a group of scarab beetles that are so powerful they are named after Greek gods such as Titan, Atlas, and Goliath.

WEIGHT

Larva weighs up to 140 g

g		50		100		150
oz	1	2	3	4	5	

g		50		100		150
oz	1	2	3	4	5	

Adult weighs up to 86 g

EGGS
Females lay from 50–100 eggs.

GROWTH
The larva takes from 1–2 years to develop into an adult beetle.

ADULT LIFESPAN 3–5 MONTHS

"A Hercules beetle can lift more than **85 times** its own body weight."

Powerful and noisy

Not only are Hercules beetles incredibly powerful, but they can also be noisy. When threatened by a predator, these beetles produce hissing squeaks by rubbing their tough wing cases against their abdomen.

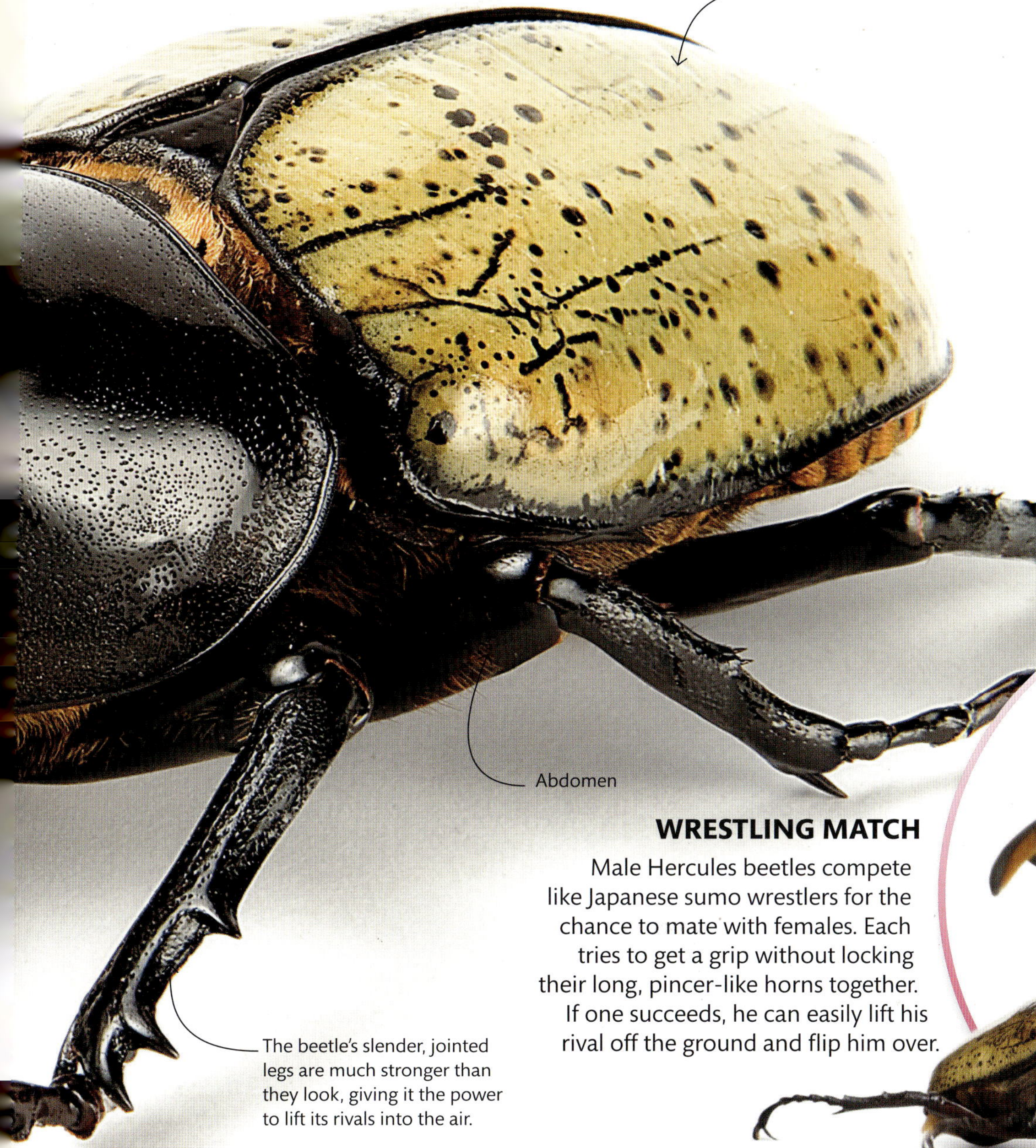
The beetle's delicate wings are protected by hard wing cases (elytra), which hinge open when the beetle takes off.
Abdomen
The beetle's slender, jointed legs are much stronger than they look, giving it the power to lift its rivals into the air.

AT A GLANCE

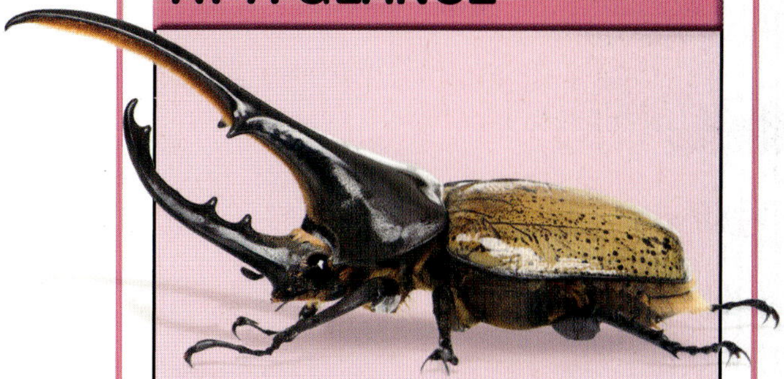

- **SIZE** Up to 17 cm (6¾ in) long
- **HABITAT** Tropical rainforest
- **LOCATION** Central and South America
- **DIET** Larva eats rotting wood; adult eats fallen fruit

WRESTLING MATCH

Male Hercules beetles compete like Japanese sumo wrestlers for the chance to mate with females. Each tries to get a grip without locking their long, pincer-like horns together. If one succeeds, he can easily lift his rival off the ground and flip him over.

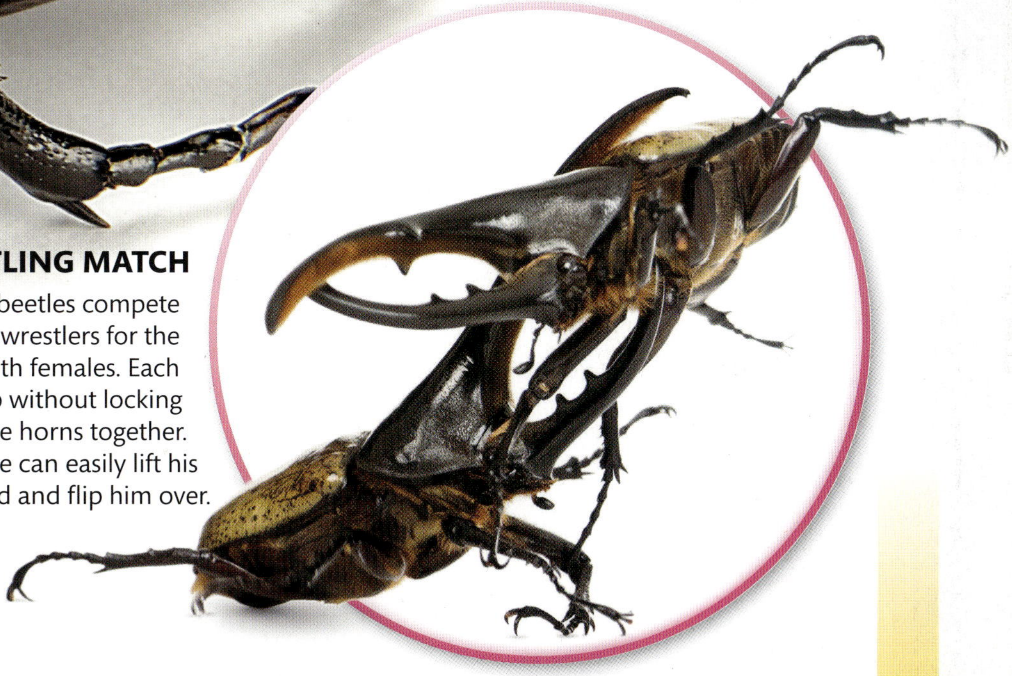

HEAVYWEIGHT CONTENDERS

A Hercules beetle weighs even more when it is a burrowing larva, feeding on dead wood. But some other tropical beetles can be even heavier provided they eat plenty of nutritious food before they turn into adults. This is because they can only grow when they are soft-bodied larvae.

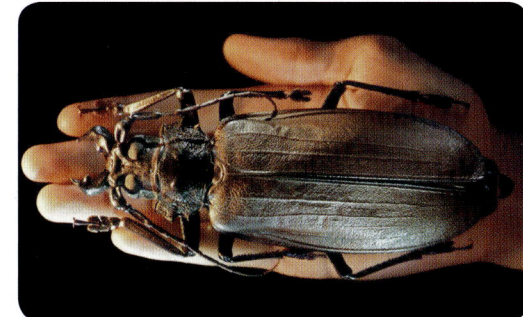

TITAN BEETLE
The South American Titan beetle is the biggest beetle on Earth. Although it is about the same length as the Hercules beetle, it has a far bigger, heavier body.

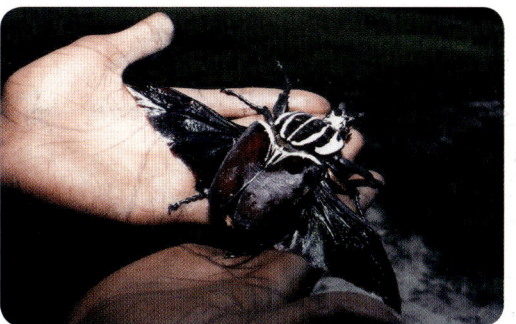

GOLIATH BEETLE
Although shorter than the Hercules beetle at up to 11 cm (4¼ in), the Central African Goliath beetle is much more heavily built, and weighs about 100 g (3½ oz).

FLYING BEETLE

Despite its weight, the Hercules beetle is well able to fly. This male has opened its rigid wing cases, revealing the delicate hind wings that propel it through the air. The beetle looks unbalanced, but the long horns are very light. The outspread wing cases may work like the wings of an aircraft, helping to generate lift as the beetle beats its hind wings and drives itself forward through the air.

"Scientists study **beetle flight** by fitting them with tiny computers."

VENOMOUS BITE
GIANT CENTIPEDE

The tropical giant centipede is a fearsome predator, able to kill a tarantula with a single venomous bite of its fang-like claws (forcipules). It is almost blind, but locates prey by scent and touch. This allows it to hunt in the dark.

The centipede chews its food with a pair of mandibles before swallowing it.

Long antennae are the centipede's main sense organs, detecting prey by both touch and scent.

Short, mobile leg-like structures called palps are used for pulling prey apart.

The forcipules are modified legs, with sharp, hollow tips for injecting venom.

Each forcipule contains a venom gland. Muscles squeeze the venom glands to force the poison into bite wounds.

The legs are adapted for speed, and move in sequence, like waves rippling down the centipede's flanks.

AT A GLANCE

- **SIZE** Up to 30 cm (12 in) long
- **HABITAT** Tropical forests
- **LOCATION** Northern South America
- **DIET** Other animals, including insects, spiders, lizards, frogs, mice, bats, and small birds

Multi-legged hunter

This is the biggest of the centipedes – a group of myriapods that have one pair of legs to each body segment. The word centipede means "100 legs", but this one has just 46. Centipedes are fast-moving hunters that favour dark, damp places, often living underground.

STATS AND FACTS

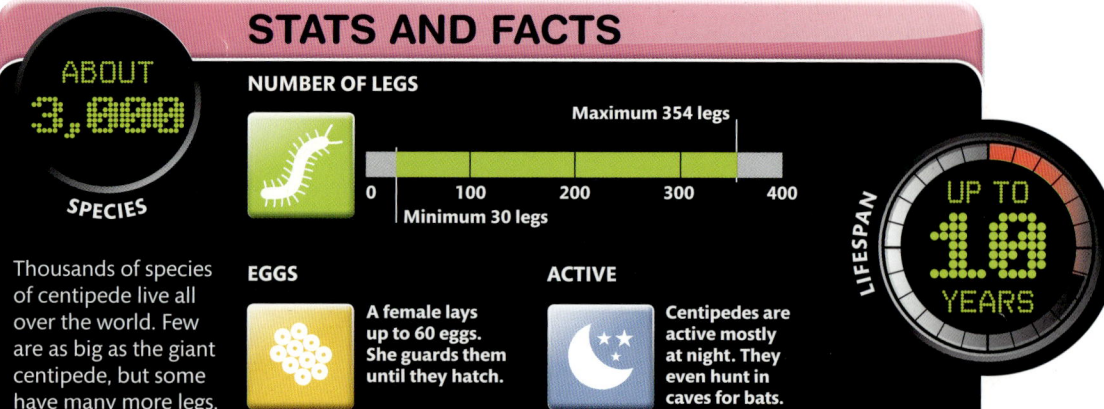

ABOUT 3,000 SPECIES

Thousands of species of centipede live all over the world. Few are as big as the giant centipede, but some have many more legs.

NUMBER OF LEGS

Maximum 354 legs

0   100   200   300   400

Minimum 30 legs

EGGS

A female lays up to 60 eggs. She guards them until they hatch.

ACTIVE

Centipedes are active mostly at night. They even hunt in caves for bats.

LIFESPAN UP TO 18 YEARS

INSECT MEAL

Seizing its prey with sharp, powerful forcipules, the centipede injects a deadly dose of venom. It holds on tight with its legs until the venom takes effect and the victim dies. The centipede then pulls the prey apart with its palps, chewing through the tough cuticle of insects. As it eats, fluid from a pair of big salivary glands starts to break down the food.

"A formidable predator, the giant centipede can even kill bats in flight."

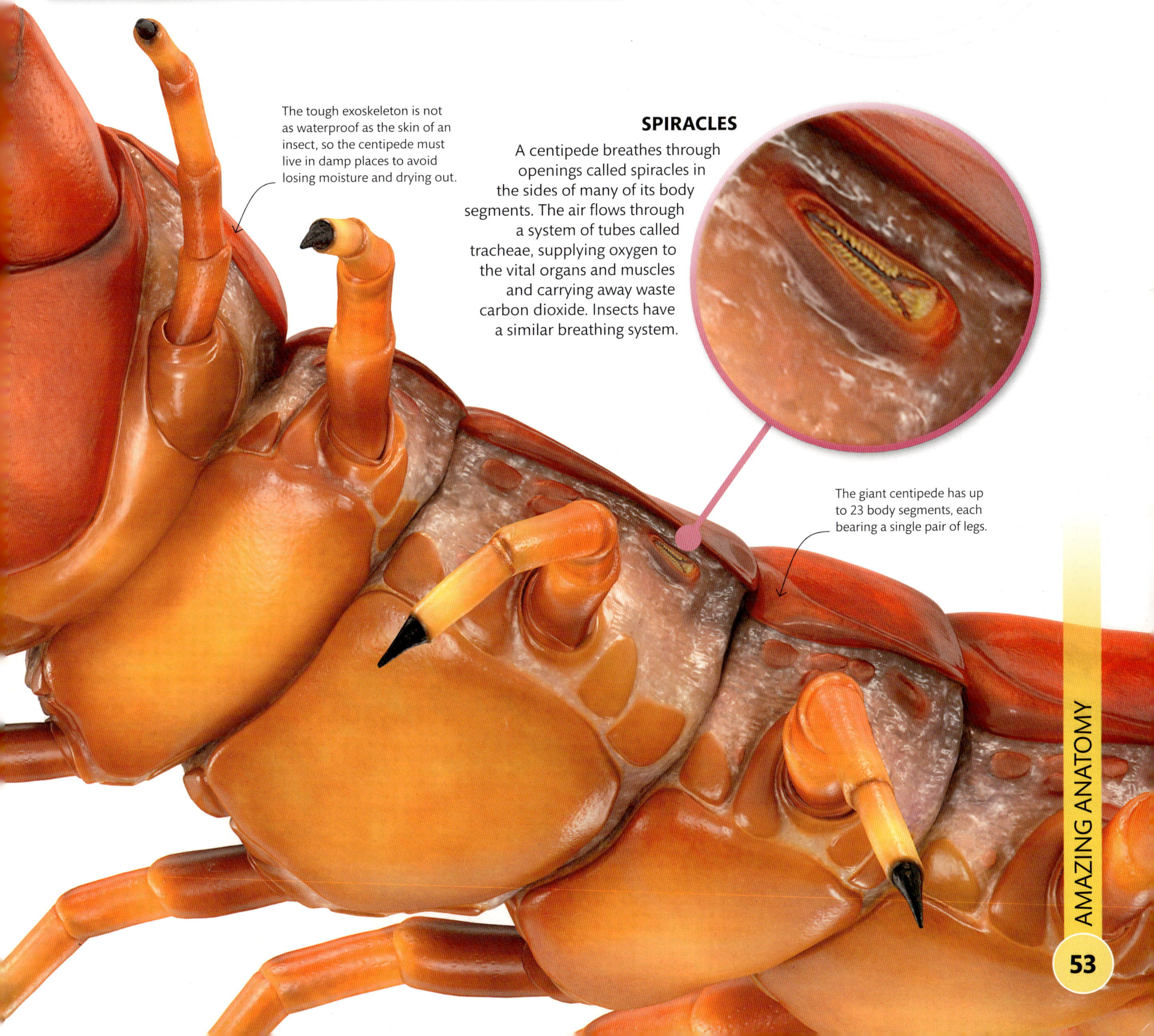

The tough exoskeleton is not as waterproof as the skin of an insect, so the centipede must live in damp places to avoid losing moisture and drying out.

SPIRACLES

A centipede breathes through openings called spiracles in the sides of many of its body segments. The air flows through a system of tubes called tracheae, supplying oxygen to the vital organs and muscles and carrying away waste carbon dioxide. Insects have a similar breathing system.

The giant centipede has up to 23 body segments, each bearing a single pair of legs.

TOXIC DIET

Glasswing butterflies feed on nectar that contains chemicals poisonous to other creatures. They can turn the poisons into substances that make the butterflies taste bad. This helps protect them from birds and other hungry predators. The caterpillars eat toxic plants that have the same effect.

SEE-THROUGH WINGS

GLASSWING BUTTERFLY

The wings of most butterflies are covered with scales that overlap like tiles on a roof. The scales give the wings their colours and patterns. But the glasswing butterfly is different. It only has scales on the edges of each wing, leaving the rest of it transparent, like glass. In fact, the wing is extra-transparent, thanks to microscopic structures that stop it reflecting light and glittering in the sunshine. This makes the butterfly almost invisible to its enemies.

AT A GLANCE

- **SIZE** Up to 3 cm (1¼ in) long, with 6 cm (2½ in) wingspan
- **HABITAT** Tropical rainforest
- **LOCATION** Central America
- **DIET** Larva eats leaves; adult sips nectar

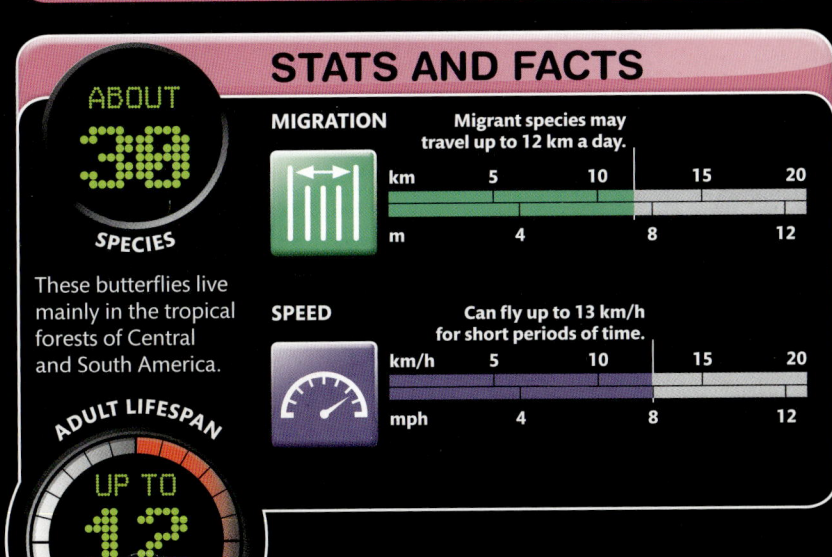

STATS AND FACTS

ABOUT 38 SPECIES

These butterflies live mainly in the tropical forests of Central and South America.

ADULT LIFESPAN UP TO 12 WEEKS

MIGRATION Migrant species may travel up to 12 km a day.

	km	5	10	15	20
	m	4	8	12	

SPEED Can fly up to 13 km/h for short periods of time.

	km/h	5	10	15	20
	mph	4	8	12	

WIDE-EYED FLY

A stalk-eyed fly hatches with eyes that are not on long stalks. To extend them, the fly pumps air into its head, making the eye-stalks extend like telescopic aerials. Both sexes have these stalks, but those of male stalk-eyed flies are much longer.

EYE-TO-EYE CONTEST
STALK-EYED FLY

The eyes of this extraordinary fly are mounted on the ends of long thin stalks. The male fly uses this unique feature to compete for females, who prefer to mate with a male that has extra-long eye-stalks because they indicate strength. Rival males know this too, and if they meet head-to-head in an eye-stalk measuring contest, the male with the shortest stalks backs down. This means that the long-stalked males father most of the young, who inherit their amazing eyes.

AT A GLANCE

- **SIZE** Body length up to 12 mm (½ in) long
- **HABITAT** Often found in humid, damp places near streams
- **LOCATION** Southeast Asia
- **DIET** Fungi and bacteria growing on decaying vegetation

STATS AND FACTS

ABOUT
150
SPECIES
These flies live in Asia and Africa, but two species are also found in North America and one in Europe.

ADULT LIFESPAN
200
DAYS

EYE-STALK LENGTH

Eyes are about 1.5 cm apart.

cm	0.5	1	1.5	2
in	¼	½	¾	

EGGS Females lay 4–6 eggs per day for up to 6 months.

VISION These incredible little flies have a 360° field of vision.

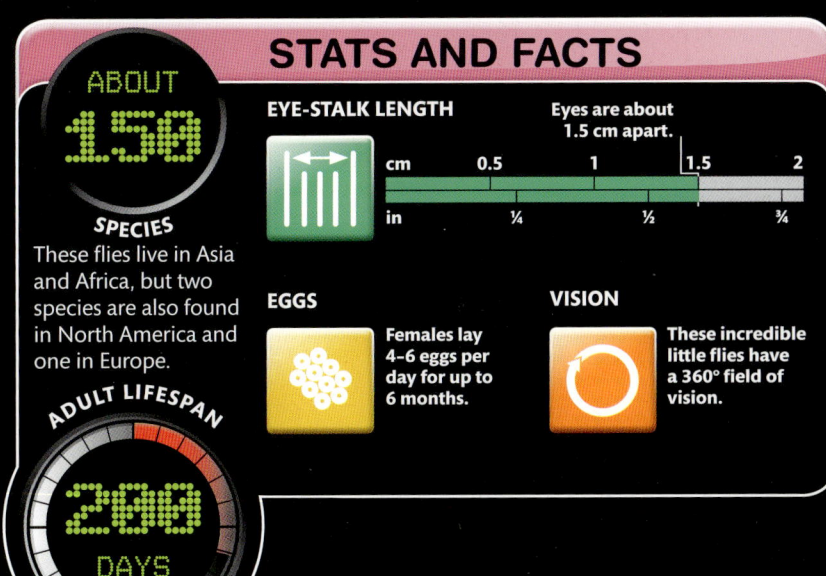

NIGHT STALKER

Like many of its relatives, this Southeast Asian vinegaroon lives in warm, damp forests, and usually hunts at night. The vinegaroon feels for prey in the dark with its long, slender front legs before seizing and crushing the victim between its claws.

ACID ATTACKER
VINEGAROON

Watch out for the whip scorpion! Often known as a vinegaroon, this fearsome-looking creature is an arachnid – an eight-legged relative of the spiders and scorpions with a long whip-like tail. It looks dangerous, with crushing claws and a menacing threat display, but it has no sting and no venomous fangs. If attacked, a vinegaroon defends itself by spraying vinegary acetic acid from a gland at the base of its slender tail, hence its name. If this acid enters enemy eyes, it causes temporary blindness, allowing the vinegaroon to make its escape.

AT A GLANCE

- **SIZE** Up to 5 cm (2 in) long, not including whip-like tail
- **HABITAT** Forests, grasslands, and deserts
- **LOCATION** Southern and Southeast Asia, North and South America, and Africa
- **DIET** Mainly insects, but also worms and slugs

STATS AND FACTS

ABOUT 100 SPECIES

Whip scorpions of this type live mainly in tropical America and the Far East.

SPRAY DISTANCE Whip scorpions can spray accurately up to 30 cm.

cm	10	20	30	40
in	4	8	12	

EGGS  A female carries up to 40 eggs in a sac under her abdomen.

ACTIVE Whip scorpions burrow or hide under debris, emerging at night to hunt.

LIFESPAN

7 YEARS

DAZZLING DECEPTION
HORNET MOTH

Warning stripes of yellow and black usually mean one thing – the risk of a painful sting. But this insect has no sting, and cannot bite. It is a harmless moth, which hungry birds mistakenly believe is a large wasp, called a hornet. Even the moth's thick antennae and transparent wings are like those of a hornet. All that is missing from this moth's superb disguise is a slender wasp waist. But the hornet moth does not need to deceive potential enemies for long. After months of life as a wood-boring caterpillar, the adult moth survives for only a few days.

AT A GLANCE

- **SIZE** Wingspan up to 48 mm (2 in)
- **HABITAT** On and near poplar and willow trees
- **LOCATION** Europe
- **DIET** Larvae burrow into poplar or willow trees, eating the timber; adults do not eat

STATS AND FACTS

ABOUT 22 SPECIES

Moths that mimic stinging wasps can be found all over the world.

GROWTH

Average lifespan in years, from larvae to adult

| years | ½ | 1 | 1½ | 2 | 2½ |

EGGS A female lays about 1,000 eggs.

ACTIVE Hornet moths are most active during the day.

ADULT LIFESPAN ABOUT 10 DAYS

"When a **harmless** creature impersonates a much **scarier** species, it is called Batesian mimicry."

SITTING PRETTY

When an adult hornet moth emerges in early summer, it spends a long time resting on a tree before taking to the air. The adult cannot eat; it only needs to live long enough to find a mate and lay eggs.

SUPER SNOUT
NUT WEEVIL

Weevils are specialized beetles that often have unusually long snouts and strange body shapes. The slender, curved snout of the female nut weevil is as long as the rest of her body – a special adaptation for boring deep holes in the hazel nuts where she lays her eggs.

The nut weevil's snout is tipped with a tiny pair of jaws for feeding and drilling into nuts.

AT A GLANCE

SIZE About 8 mm (¼ in)

HABITAT Hazel trees in woodland

LOCATION Europe

DIET Hazel nuts, buds, and leaves

NUT DRILL

The nut weevil is one of several closely related species that are specially adapted for drilling into nuts. This one favours acorns – the seeds of oak trees.

STATS AND FACTS

ABOUT 60,000 SPECIES

Weevils are found all over the world. Most species are adapted for eating just one type of plant.

EGGS

Each female can lay up to 30 eggs.

0   5   10   15   20   25   30   35

CROP PESTS

Many weevils damage crops such as rice.

HOUSE PESTS

Weevils are also found in cereal and flour.

ADULT LIFESPAN 2–3 MONTHS

"The snout length and shape varies greatly depending on the species."

Strong legs with clawed feet are ideal for scrambling through foliage.

Tree of life

The nut weevil spends its entire life on one type of plant – hazel trees. The adult weevils feed on the buds and leaves, and the females lay their eggs in the nuts. The hatching larvae eat the nuts, then emerge and burrow into the ground to turn into adults.

WEIRD WEEVILS

Many weevils have unusual body shapes, bright colours and patterns, or are covered with tufts of hair-like bristles.

BLUE WEEVIL
Found in the tropical rainforests of New Guinea, the blue weevil is covered with tiny, ridged scales that glitter iridescent blue-green in shafts of sunlight.

RED PALM WEEVIL
This big, rusty-red weevil is one of many species that have become pests of cultivated plants. Its larvae bore deep holes in palm trees, eventually killing them.

LARINUS WEEVIL
The hairy body of *Larinus sturnus* (like many weevils, it has no common name) is dappled with bright yellow patches. It lives in the grassy meadows of Europe.

HAIRY WEEVIL
The brightly coloured bristles sprouting from the back of this Madagascan weevil may help it to attract a mate.

SUPER-THIN BODY

VIOLIN BEETLE

Many small creatures live under the loose bark of dead trees, where they are hidden from hungry birds. But there is no safety in the forests of Southeast Asia. Here, they are targeted by an insect perfectly adapted to hunt them – the violin beetle. With its flattened body, the beetle slips beneath flaking bark and sprouting fungi, and uses its narrow head to probe cracks in the timber for insect grubs and snails. Feeling in the dark with very long, sensitive antennae, the beetle seizes its prey with sharp, curved jaws.

AT A GLANCE

- **SIZE** Up to 10 cm (4 in) long
- **HABITAT** Rainforest trees
- **LOCATION** Southeast Asia
- **DIET** Insects and snails

STATS AND FACTS

ABOUT 5 SPECIES

So-called because of their violin-shaped body, all five species are found in Southeast Asia.

ADULT LIFESPAN 2-3 YEARS

DEFENCE
To deter a predator, the violin beetle secretes a smelly fluid from its glands.

ACTIVE
This species is a night-time hunter.

GROWTH
Larvae take up to nine months to develop.

months
1 2 3 4 5 6 7 8 9 10 11 12

INVISIBLE INTRUDER

The broad, flattened elytra (forewings) of the violin beetle are so thin that they are almost transparent. They make it hard to spot this hunter as it scuttles across the fallen leaves of the forest floor.

HAIRY WINGS

While some fairyflies are wingless or are short-winged, many have extraordinary wings that are fringed with long hairs. The wings may look useless for flying, but the mechanics of flight are different for such tiny creatures, and they can fly perfectly well.

SMALLEST FLYING INSECT

MIND-BLOWINGLY SMALL
FAIRYFLY

Named for their delicate frame, tiny size, and feathery-looking wings, fairyflies are actually tiny wasps – the smallest of all flying insects. They are so small that they breed by laying their eggs inside the tiny eggs of other insects. When the wasp grub hatches, it feeds on the egg until it is ready to turn into an adult. The adults have very short lives, and many do not feed at all, devoting their time to finding a mate and breeding. In one species from Costa Rica, the minuscule male is the smallest insect on Earth.

AT A GLANCE

- **SIZE** Up to 5.4 mm (¼ in) long, but most are much smaller at 0.5–1.0 mm (⅕₀–⅕₂₅ in)

- **HABITAT** Widespread in all habitats; some are even aquatic

- **LOCATION** Worldwide, except polar regions

- **DIET** Larvae eat insect eggs; adults drink sugary nectar or honeydew, or do not eat at all

STATS AND FACTS

ABOUT 1,400 SPECIES

Fairyflies live almost everywhere, but are so small that we rarely notice them.

ADULT LIFESPAN
1–15 DAYS

RECORD BREAKER
The smallest species is a quarter the size of a full stop.

EGGS
The female lays up to 100 eggs.

ACTIVE
Fairyflies are active during the day. They are usually solitary insects.

WATER BUGS
Aquatic species use their wings to swim around.

LONGEST TONGUE
MORGAN'S SPHINX MOTH

This Madagascan moth has a longer tongue than any other insect. The moth needs it to reach into a white star-shaped orchid that hides its sweet nectar at the end of a very long tube. The orchid has a very intense sweet fragrance, which is only released at night, and this attracts the moth from a considerable distance. As no other insect can reach into the orchid's nectar store, the moth has a guaranteed food supply.

The sphinx moth is a powerful flier with long wings.

Instead of hovering to feed, the moth uses its legs to cling to the flower.

Sweet treat

Landing on the orchid, the moth slips its long tongue deep into the flower spur to drink the nectar. When it has finished, it flies off to find another flower of the same type. In the process, the moth carries pollen from one orchid plant directly to another. This pollinates the orchid so it can set seed.

White petals are visible in the dark.

The flower spur is a narrow tube, just wide enough for the moth's tongue.

Moth's long, slender tongue

"The moth's tongue is more than five times the length of its body"

NEAT COIL

When the sphinx moth's incredibly long tongue is not reaching inside a flower, it is rolled up under the insect's head in a flat coil. The tubular tongue works like a drinking straw, sucking up the sugary liquid.

AT A GLANCE

SIZE About 6.5 cm (2½ in) long, without tongue

HABITAT Tropical forests

LOCATION Madagascar and East Africa

DIET Adult moth drinks nectar; caterpillar eats leaves

The nectar is hidden deep at the end of the flower spur; only a sphinx moth can reach it.

DELIVERY SERVICE

1

2

3

The orchid has a good reason for attracting the moth – it needs an insect to carry pollen to another orchid of the same species. The pollen is contained in two tiny capsules, and as the moth pulls out of the flower, the capsules become attached to the base of its very long tongue.

Tongue coiled tight, with the pollen capsules still attached, the moth prepares to fly off in search of another orchid. It is not interested in other types of flower, so there is no risk that the moth will deliver the pollen to the wrong plant. It is doing exactly what the orchid needs it to do.

When it finds another orchid, the moth unrolls its tongue to sip the nectar. As it starts feeding, the capsules of pollen transfer to the new flower, fertilizing it so that it can make seeds. The orchid's winged messenger has done its work and earned another sweet reward for all the effort.

STATS AND FACTS

ACTIVE

Sphinx moths and hawk moths are nocturnal insects, feeding at night.

DEFENCE

When resting by day, these moths are camouflaged, protecting them from predators.

RECORD BREAKER

The moth's tongue stretches to 35 cm (14 in).

WINGBEAT

Sphinx moths are strong, fast fliers, with very fast wingbeats.

ABOUT 1,450

SPECIES

Morgan's sphinx moth is one of many hawk moths found all over the world.

ADULT LIFESPAN

ABOUT 18 WEEKS

GLITTERING GOLD BUGS
GOLDEN CHAFER

Some of the world's most beautiful beetles are jewel scarabs, known for their striking colours and shiny bodies that seem to be made of metal. This metallic effect is caused by light reflecting through the specially layered structure of their body armour. Many of them glitter green or red, but the golden chafer from Central America is tinted yellow, making it look like it is made of solid gold. Surprisingly, this sheen makes the beetle harder to see, because the reflections conceal its shape among the wet, sunlit leaves of its tropical rainforest home.

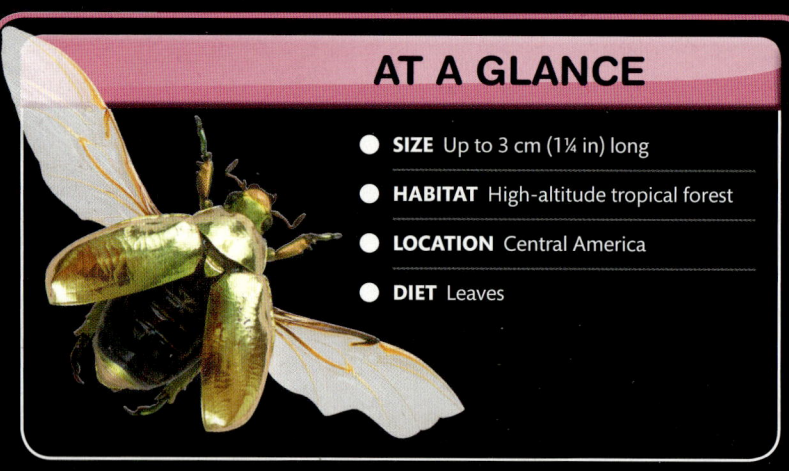

AT A GLANCE

- **SIZE** Up to 3 cm (1¼ in) long
- **HABITAT** High-altitude tropical forest
- **LOCATION** Central America
- **DIET** Leaves

STATS AND FACTS

ABOUT 65 SPECIES

Jewel beetles are found only in South and Central America and in southwest USA.

ADULT LIFESPAN ABOUT 3 MONTHS

ACTIVE
Active mostly at night, and is also attracted to bright lights.

DEFENCE
In the sunlight, the shiny body helps to confuse predators.

HIGHLY PRIZED
A gold jewel beetle can fetch as much as £300 among collectors.

STATUS
Threatened by habitat destruction and by collectors.

GOLD DIGGER

The golden chafer is perfectly adapted for burrowing in the ground. Using its broad, spade-shaped front legs, the beetle easily pushes the soil aside.

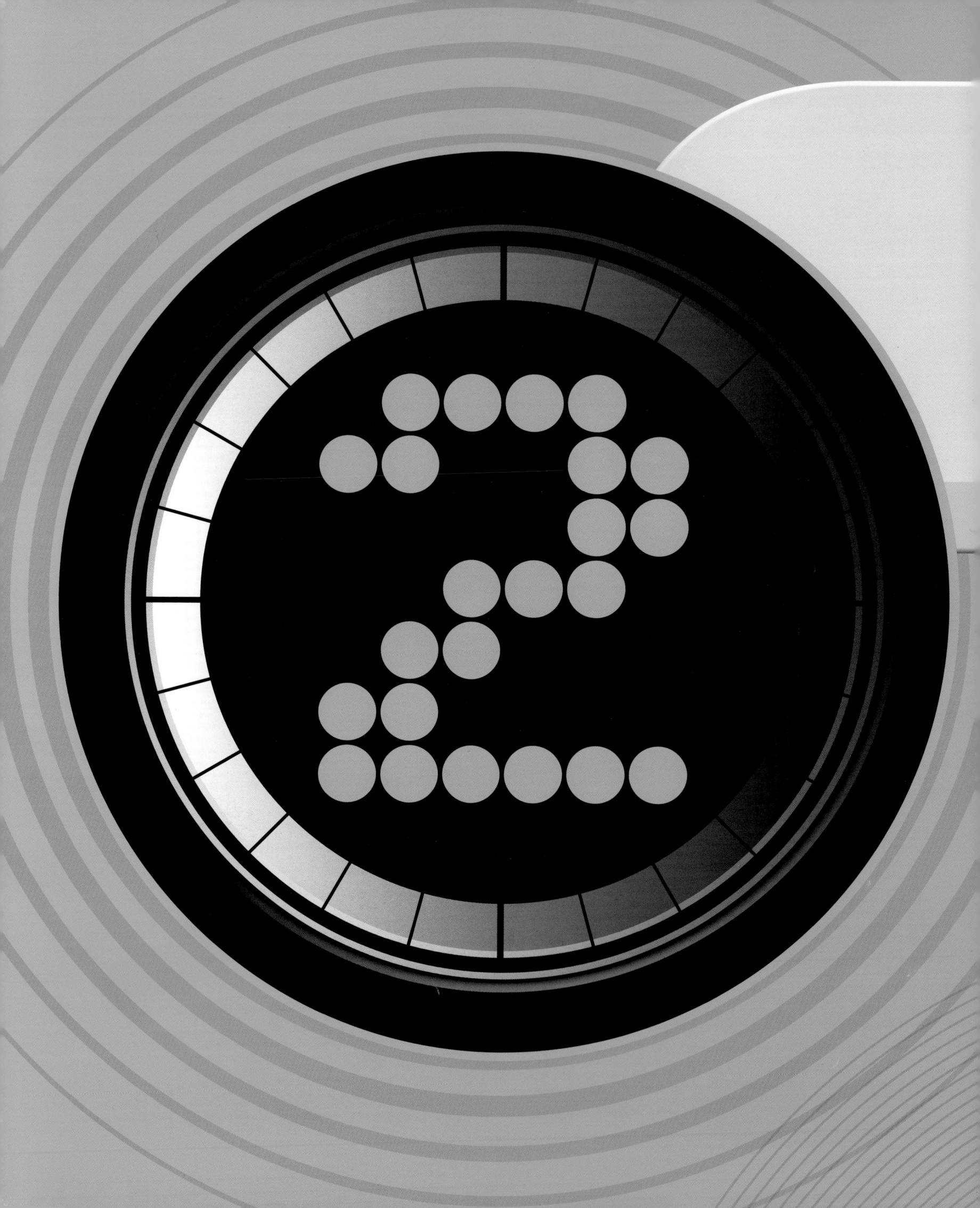

ANIMAL ATHLETES

Whether they are running, jumping, or flying, bugs are real record breakers. Despite their tiny size, some can move at mind-boggling speeds, while others achieve amazing feats of agility on the ground or in the air. Many bugs use these skills to hunt, feed, or escape danger.

LONGEST MIGRATION

THE BIG SLEEP

In winter, vast numbers of monarchs gather in the warm woodlands of California and Mexico. They stay for more than four months, sleeping in dense clusters on favoured trees, before heading north again to breed.

INCREDIBLE JOURNEY
MONARCH BUTTERFLIES

Butterflies appear fragile as they flutter between flowers, gathering nectar. But some butterflies are capable of amazingly long flights, crossing continents and even flying across oceans. The North American monarch holds the distance record – successive generations gradually move northeast across America to the Canadian border in summer, but the final generation flies all the way back to California and Mexico to spend the winter. This means that a single monarch butterfly may fly 4,800 km (3,000 miles).

AT A GLANCE

- **SIZE** Wingspan up to 11 cm (4¼ in)
- **HABITAT** Warm woodlands in winter; rough grassland in summer
- **LOCATION** Native to North America and northern South America; also Australia and New Zealand
- **DIET** Adult butterflies drink nectar; caterpillars feed on milkweed foliage

STATS AND FACTS

12

SPECIES

Most monarchs live for about a month, but the ones that sleep over winter live for up to eight months.

DISTANCE

80 km per day is covered when flying south.

km	10	20	30	40	50	60	70	80	90
miles	10		20		30		40		50

FLYING SOUTH

Up to 300 million monarch butterflies migrate every year.

EGGS

A female may lay up to 1,200 eggs.

WEIGHT

UP TO
0.75
GRAMS

CHAMPION JUMPER
FROGHOPPER

This brown froghopper may not look very special, but it is one of nature's champion athletes. Compared to its size this bug can jump higher than any other animal, and in the process survives forces that would kill a human. The froghopper achieves this feat with a special set of muscles that store energy like a catapult. When suddenly released, these hurl the insect into the air.

Front of head contains big muscles for sucking plant sap.

Big compound eyes allow the bug to watch for possible danger.

AT A GLANCE

SIZE 6 mm (¼ in) long

HABITAT Woodlands, grasslands, and gardens

LOCATION Europe, Asia, North America, and New Zealand

DIET Plant sap

Sap-sucker

A froghopper is a type of true bug – an insect that feeds by sucking up liquids with a set of tubular mouthparts. Like many other true bugs, it drinks the sugary sap of grasses and other plants. It can run and fly, but escapes danger by jumping.

STATS AND FACTS

ABOUT

2,500

SPECIES

Froghoppers are very adaptable, and live on many different types of plants growing all over the world.

RECORD BREAKER

Can leap 70 cm into the air.

cm	20	40	60	80
in	8	16	24	

TAKE-OFF

Take-off speed has been calculated to be 4 m/sec.

m/sec	2	4	6
ft/sec	6	12	18

ADULT LIFESPAN

3-4 MONTHS

"Accelerates with a **force** *that is* **400** *times the force of gravity."*

BUBBLE NEST

Female froghoppers lay their eggs on plants. When they hatch, the young nymphs feed on sap like their parents, but hide from hungry birds by feasting inside a nest of foam. They make this by blowing air through a waste fluid to create a mass of bubbles.

The white foam is sometimes called cuckoo-spit.

Wings are folded over the body like a roof when not needed.

Legs have the strength needed to launch the froghopper into the air without breaking.

TAKING OFF

Two huge muscles in the froghopper's body power the back legs. They store energy like compressed springs, ready for action.

COUNTDOWN
When the froghopper senses danger it crouches and locks its back legs in a folded position, meanwhile tensing the massive muscles that drive them.

IGNITION
Within a second the muscles build up enough power to make the locks on the back legs snap open. The legs spring straight in less than a millisecond.

LIFT-OFF
The sudden thrust launches the froghopper into the air; it accelerates with 80 times the G-force that is experienced by astronauts being blasted into Space.

Long hind legs suddenly extend, hurling the flea more than 30 cm (12 in) into the air.

FLYING FLEA

The tiny bloodsucking fleas that prey on cats and other animals use a similar mechanism to leap on to their victims. Big muscles inside a flea's body squeeze pads made of a springy substance called resilin, storing the energy needed for the leap. The energy is locked in the pads until a trigger releases it, making the flea's legs snap down and catapulting it into the air.

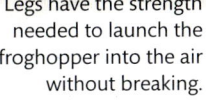

PERFECT FLIGHT CONTROL
HOVER FLY

Most insects have two pairs of wings, but a fly has just one working pair. Despite this, many flies are incredibly agile in the air. The most skilled are the hover flies that can dart forwards, backwards, or sideways, and hover on the spot as if locked in place – all thanks to a pair of special flight control organs called halteres.

Long, narrow wings are ideally shaped for the fly's fast, agile flight style.

Bold yellow and black stripes make the hover fly look like a small wasp.

Flight control
This slender, nectar-feeding hover fly is superbly adapted for flight. The fly's wings are only small, but they are controlled by an amazingly effective guidance system. This enables the insect to go exactly where it wants within seconds, without being swept off course by the wind.

Despite the wasp-like stripes, this insect has no sting. It cannot bite, and is actually harmless.

AT A GLANCE

- **SIZE** Up to 18 mm (¾ in) long
- **HABITAT** Woodlands, grasslands, and gardens
- **LOCATION** Worldwide except Antarctica
- **DIET** Adults drink nectar; larvae eat decaying plant or animal matter, or other insects

BEE OR HOVER FLY?
Many hover flies have striped bodies that look similar to wasps or bees. The honey bee and hover fly on the right look almost identical. This is a form of mimicry. It makes birds and other predators hesitate before attacking an insect that might have a painful sting – giving the hover fly a chance to escape.

Honey bee   **Hover fly**

Short antennae sense changes in wind speed, working with the halteres to achieve perfect flight control.

Huge compound eyes give the fly the sharp vision it needs for flight, and to spot potential mates or rivals.

Thorax is packed with muscles that power both the wings and the halteres.

The halteres are attached where other insects have a second pair of wings.

Haltere

STATS AND FACTS

ABOUT
6,000

SPECIES

Hover flies live in any location where there are flowers to feed on.

DEFENCE

Mimicry of stinging insects discourages enemies that hunt by sight, such as insect-eating birds.

ACTIVE

Hover flies are active during the day. Like bees, they are important pollinators of flowering plants.

FLIGHT SPEED

A hover fly can reach speeds of up to 3.5 m/sec (almost 12 ft/sec).

GROWTH

It takes about 25–30 days for an egg to become an adult fly. Many hover fly larvae eat plant pests.

LIFESPAN

UP TO
6
WEEKS

ON AUTOPILOT

The hindwings of a hover fly – and any true fly – are reduced to tiny club-shaped halteres that beat rapidly in flight. Sensors at their bases detect if the fly has veered off track, and send a signal to the wing muscles to make a correction, very much like an aircraft autopilot.

AGILE ATTACKER
JUMPING SPIDER

Many spiders build webs to trap their prey and never go hunting; a lot of them are almost blind. But the tiny jumping spiders are very different. Targeting insects with their enormous, efficient eyes they creep up on prey and leap into the attack like miniature tigers.

Back legs provide the power for jumping. The legs are extended by having fluid forced into them.

The safety line is spun from extra-strong silk.

SAFETY LINE

All spiders make silk, using it to spin webs, make nests, and weave nurseries for their young. But a jumping spider has another use for it. Like a rock climber, this spider only makes risky moves when attached to a silk safety line – so if something goes wrong, there isn't far to fall.

Powerful front legs are used to seize prey.

Deadly jump

Jumping spiders are agile hunters with several different types of eyes that are adapted for detecting and targeting prey. When the spider spots a possible meal, such as a fly, it creeps closer until it is within range, then suddenly launches itself into the air to pounce on its victim and kill it with a venomous bite.

AT A GLANCE

- **SIZE** Up to 22 mm (1 in) long
- **HABITAT** From woodlands to scrublands, gardens, and mountainous areas
- **LOCATION** Worldwide
- **DIET** Insects and other spiders

DANCE DISPLAY

Jumping spiders have such good vision that colours and patterns are very important to them – especially when they perform their courtship displays. The male Australian peacock spider even has two vividly coloured flaps on his abdomen that he raises during his courtship dance. He waves his white-tipped third pair of legs in the air for added impact, and may keep up the display for 30 minutes or more.

The big central pair of eyes give the spider a detailed view of its target.

The two smaller front-facing eyes have a wide field of vision, which the spider uses to scan for moving prey.

WEB WARRIOR

So small that it is almost lost on this coin, the fringed jumping spider is one of the most fearless hunters on Earth. It specializes in attacking and eating web-building spiders, which are often larger than itself and could easily kill it. Sneaking on to a web, the spider plucks on the silk to lure its prey closer, before jumping on top of it and biting hard.

Body and legs bristle with sensory hairs that detect air movements.

STATS AND FACTS

MORE THAN 5,000 SPECIES

Although most jumping spiders are found in the tropics, one species can even be found on the slopes of Mount Everest.

EXTENT OF JUMP
Some jumpimg spiders can leap up to 30 times their body length.

DEFENCE
These spiders have sharp vision to spot danger, and many are camouflaged.

RECORD BREAKER
The Himalayan jumping spider is the highest-living land animal.

ACTIVE
Jumping spiders mainly hunt during the day.

LIFESPAN 12 MONTHS

"Jumping spiders are **intelligent hunters**, able to learn from experience."

SUPER SIGHT

Compared to its body, a jumping spider's main eyes are huge. Their big, single lenses are fixed, but the eye structure behind them can move to target prey precisely. The eyes act like binoculars, detecting every detail. They also allow the spider to judge distances accurately, so it knows exactly how far to jump. The other eyes see less detail, but they have a much wider field of view.

LONG REACH

The hummingbird hawkmoth's very long proboscis allows it to reach deep inside tubular flowers. Since most other insects cannot do this, these flowers are likely to contain a lot of nectar. This is why the hawkmoth is so selective, zipping from one long-flowered plant to the next.

EXPERT HOVERER
HUMMINGBIRD HAWKMOTH

Most moths are active at night, but some fly by day. One of the most eyecatching is the hummingbird hawkmoth. Darting from flower to flower, sipping nectar while hovering, the hawkmoth looks and behaves just like a tiny hummingbird. The wings even hum in the same way. The moth can also fly very fast, enabling it to make long non-stop journeys over the sea as it migrates from Africa to northern Europe and Britain in summer.

AT A GLANCE

- **SIZE** Wingspan up to 5 cm (2 in)
- **HABITAT** Woodland, flower-rich grassland, and gardens
- **LOCATION** Europe, Asia, and North Africa
- **DIET** Adult drinks nectar; caterpillar eats leaves of bedstraw or madder plants

STATS AND FACTS

ABOUT
110
SPECIES

This is one of many similar species, most of which live in Southeast Asia.

ADULT LIFESPAN
UP TO
4
MONTHS

EGGS

The female lays up to 200 eggs, each on a separate plant.

WINGBEATS

Hummingbird hawkmoths beat their wings up to 80 times a second.

PROBOSCIS

With a length of up to 2.8 cm, this moth has a longer proboscis than any other European flower-visiting insect.

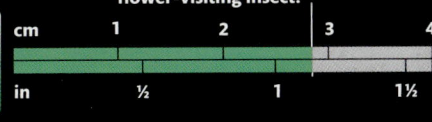

	cm	1	2	3	4
	in	½	1		1½

SUPER SPRINTER
HOUSE CENTIPEDE

Built for speed, the long-legged house centipede is specialized for chasing insects and spiders across open surfaces. The flat walls and floors of houses make ideal hunting grounds. Like all centipedes, this one thrives best in damp places. It favours cellars and bathrooms, often alarming people by darting out of hiding to seize prey with its venomous claws.

All legs

Most centipedes have about 35 pairs of legs. But the house centipede just has 15. The legs are exceptionally long and get steadily longer from head to tail, so the centipede's feet do not get in a tangle as it runs. They move in waves like the legs of all centipedes, but much faster, and few small animals can outrun such a speedy hunter.

The long legs have dark bands that match the stripes on the body.

Long, slender antennae detect prey by scent and touch.

Compound eyes

The sharp-tipped claws are used to inject venom into its prey.

COMPOUND EYES

The house centipede has excellent sight. Its complicated compound eyes, made up of many separate lenses, see a lot more than the clusters of small, simple eyes (ocelli) found in other types of centipede. Despite this superior vision, the house centipede mostly hunts at night, relying on its sensitive antennae to locate prey.

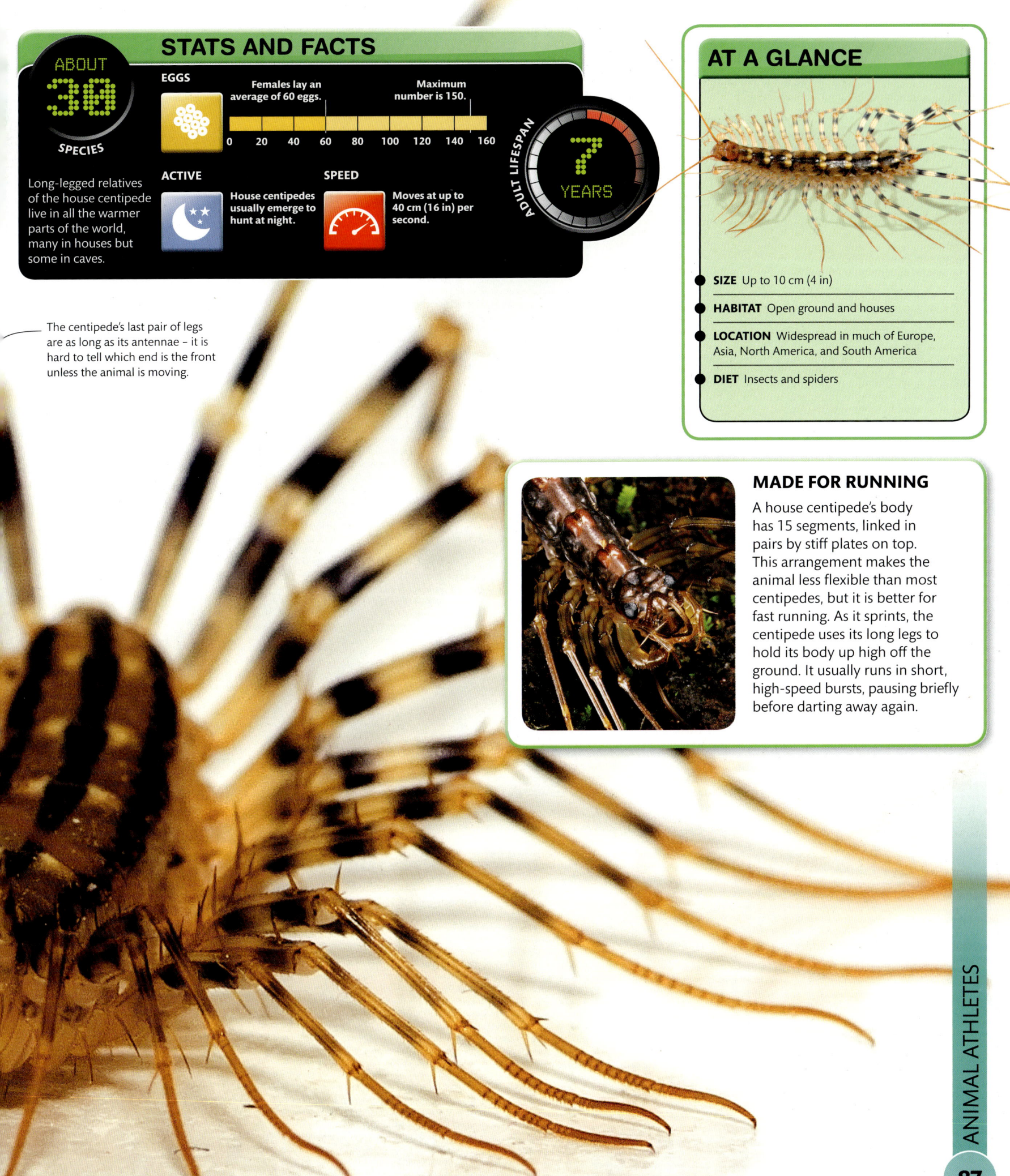

STATS AND FACTS

ABOUT 38 SPECIES

Long-legged relatives of the house centipede live in all the warmer parts of the world, many in houses but some in caves.

EGGS

Females lay an average of 60 eggs. Maximum number is 150.

| 0 | 20 | 40 | 60 | 80 | 100 | 120 | 140 | 160 |

ACTIVE

House centipedes usually emerge to hunt at night.

SPEED

Moves at up to 40 cm (16 in) per second.

ADULT LIFESPAN

7 YEARS

The centipede's last pair of legs are as long as its antennae – it is hard to tell which end is the front unless the animal is moving.

AT A GLANCE

- **SIZE** Up to 10 cm (4 in)
- **HABITAT** Open ground and houses
- **LOCATION** Widespread in much of Europe, Asia, North America, and South America
- **DIET** Insects and spiders

MADE FOR RUNNING

A house centipede's body has 15 segments, linked in pairs by stiff plates on top. This arrangement makes the animal less flexible than most centipedes, but it is better for fast running. As it sprints, the centipede uses its long legs to hold its body up high off the ground. It usually runs in short, high-speed bursts, pausing briefly before darting away again.

FASTEST RUNNER

GLITTERING GREEN
The iridescent green body of the tiger beetle glitters in the summer sunshine as it darts over open ground in pursuit of prey. Long, sensitive antennae are used to detect and avoid any obstacles.

LIFE IN THE FAST LANE
TIGER BEETLE

Tiger beetles are among the fastest runners on the planet, relative to their size. These speed demons can rocket across the ground at up to 9 km/h (5 mph), which works out at 125 times their own body length every second. By comparison, the cheetah – the fastest land animal on Earth, reaching 120 km/h (75 mph) – covers just 23 body lengths a second. The tiger beetle uses this incredible speed to catch its prey. It runs so fast that its surroundings become a blur, but the beetle has plenty of time to stop and check that it is still on target.

AT A GLANCE

- **SIZE** 12–15 mm (½ in) in length
- **HABITAT** Open ground with dry, sandy, or chalky soil
- **LOCATION** Europe and Asia
- **DIET** Insects and spiders

STATS AND FACTS

ABOUT 2,600 SPECIES

Different species of tiger beetle live all over the world, mainly in sandy habitats.

LIFESPAN: LARVA TO ADULT

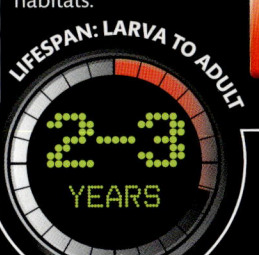

2–3 YEARS

RECORD BREAKER

A small species of tiger beetle in Australia can cover 2.5 m in 1 second.

m		1	2	3
ft	3	6	9	

DEFENCE These beetles fly fast and bite hard.

ACTIVE Runs and flies readily and is most active in the heat of the day.

JAWS OF DEATH

Equipped with the sharpest eyesight of any beetle, the green tiger beetle uses its big, bulging compound eyes to spot victims, give chase, and catch prey. A pair of hugely powerful toothed jaws slice through the prey's tough armour, before the beetle smothers its meal in digestive juices to soften the flesh. Then it's time to devour dinner.

ULTIMATE SURVIVOR

TARDIGRADE

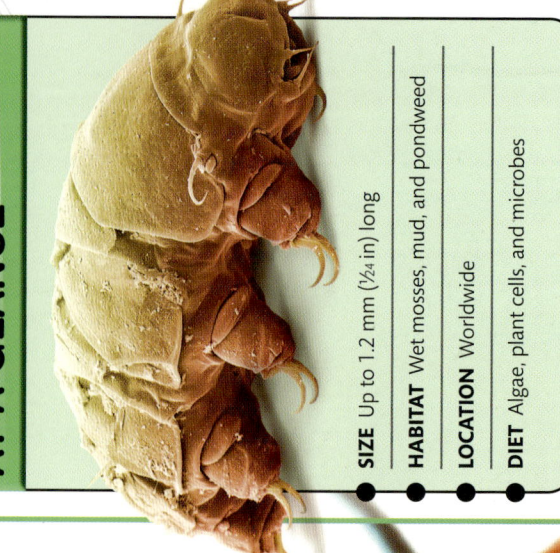

SIZE Up to 1.2 mm (¹⁄₂₄ in) long

HABITAT Wet mosses, mud, and pondweed

LOCATION Worldwide

DIET Algae, plant cells, and microbes

This miniature marvel is one of the smallest animals on Earth, but also one of the toughest. No bigger than a grain of salt, it lives in damp, mossy places and ponds where it feeds on plant fluids and microbes. But if its habitat dries up, the tardigrade can survive for years in a dehydrated state that would kill any other animal. Incredibly, once it gets wet again, and within just a few minutes, the tardigrade revives and starts feeding as if nothing has happened.

DRY TUN

If the tardigrade runs out of food and water, its body dries up and shrinks into a shapeless bundle called a tun. In this state it can survive extreme cold, scalding heat, and 1,000 times the normal lethal level of radioactivity. Tardigrades have even survived being sent into Space.

Water bear

A tardigrade has eight short, stumpy legs and a rounded, bulky body. Under a microscope the shape resembles a tiny bear as it searches its watery home for food, so it is sometimes called a water bear. The tardigrade feeds by piercing the tough-walled cells of plants or microbes to release the juices inside.

STARRY EGGS

Tardigrades reproduce by laying eggs. Each egg has a hard shell shaped like a starburst. It usually hatches after two weeks, but can survive for many months.

Stout sensory bristles detect nearby objects and air movements.

The hard shell protects the egg from drying out.

The body is protected by flexible skin, similar to the skin of a caterpillar.

Short, soft-skinned legs do not have joints, and can flex in any direction.

Each leg has a cluster of sharp claws and a sticky pad for extra grip.

Tubular mouth is armed with sharp stylets for piercing the cells it feeds on.

SMALL WONDERS

Tardigrades are not the only tiny creatures with amazing survival powers. The microscopic bdelloid rotifers that live in ponds and other fresh waters have the same ability to dry up like a dead leaf but still stay alive, reviving when conditions improve. They have been known to survive for up to nine years like this. Their bodies have an amazing ability to repair the damage caused by the drying out, using genetic material obtained from the bacteria and other microbes they eat.

STATS AND FACTS

ABOUT

900

SPECIES

Tardigrades can be found in every type of habitat, from tropical forests to snowy polar areas.

EGGS

A female lays up to 30 eggs at a time. These too can survive months with no moisture.

TEMPERATURE TOLERATION

Tardigrades can survive extreme temperatures of –200°C to 151°C (–328°F to 304°F).

WATER CONTENT

Body water content drops to 3% as a tun.

When active, it is 85%.

0% 20% 40% 60% 80% 100%

LIFESPAN IN TUN STATE

49 YEARS

ANIMAL ATHLETES

UNLIKELY AERONAUT
BUMBLE BEE

Big, furry bumble bees have surprisingly small wings, and someone once calculated that, compared to a bumble bee's weight, its wing area is not big enough to keep it airborne. But this false calculation was based on the way birds fly, which is not how a bee flies. Instead of beating its wings up and down, the bee beats them forward and back. This makes the wings flex and rotate, generating swirling eddies in the air that create lift above each wing. The process works so well that the bee's wings can be much smaller, relative to its weight.

AT A GLANCE

- **SIZE** Up to 2 cm (¾ in) long
- **HABITAT** Woodlands, grasslands, and gardens
- **LOCATION** Europe, western Asia, and North Africa
- **DIET** Adult drinks nectar; young are fed on nectar and pollen

STATS AND FACTS

ABOUT
250
SPECIES

Bumble bees are found almost worldwide, apart from Australia and most of Africa.

COLONY

Bumble bees live in colonies of 50–400 bees; like honey bees, they have one queen.

UNDERGROUND NEST

Most species nest in underground cavities, such as empty mouse holes.

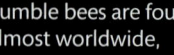

DEFENCE

The bees have a sting, but rarely use it except to defend their nest.

WINGBEATS

A bumble bee beats its wings about 200 times per second.

WORKER BEE'S LIFESPAN
ABOUT 6 WEEKS

"A single worker bumble bee may visit **200,000** flowers in its lifetime."

IN FLIGHT

This buff-tailed bumble bee is a flying acrobat, able to hover beneath a flower when looking for nectar to drink. The bee visits thousands of flowers in its lifetime and, in the process, carries the vital pollen that fertilizes flowers and enables them to make seeds.

DYNAMIC DIGGER

The mole cricket has a pair of strong, spade-like front legs for digging. Its other legs are shorter than those of most crickets, and its body is almost cylindrical, enabling the cricket to slip swiftly through tunnels.

MUSICAL EXCAVATOR
MOLE CRICKET

Built like a miniature bulldozer, the mole cricket is perfectly equipped for a life spent burrowing through the soil, creating a network of tunnels for feeding, breeding, and even singing. In spring, the male digs a special burrow to broadcast his courtship song far and wide. Built like twin flared horns with a tuned chamber, the burrow amplifies his rasping call into a deep, penetrating churring that may attract a female mole cricket up to 2 km (1.2 miles) away.

AT A GLANCE

- **SIZE** Up to 5 cm (2 in) long
- **HABITAT** Damp grasslands and fields
- **LOCATION** Europe and western Asia
- **DIET** Roots, insects, grubs, and worms

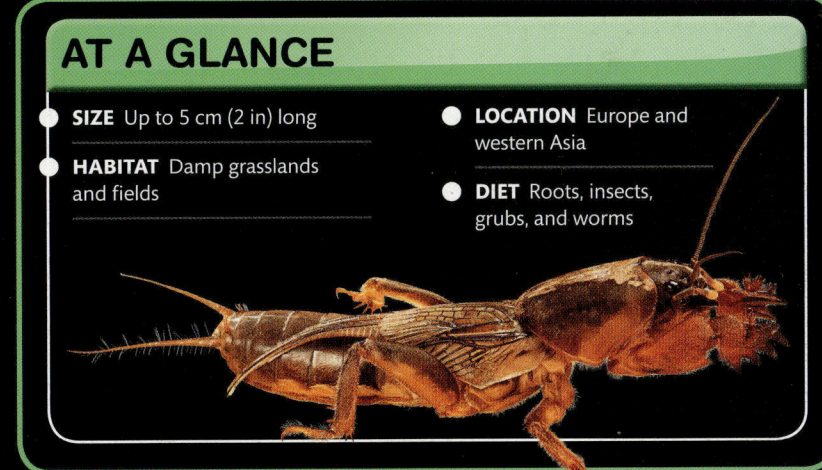

STATS AND FACTS

ABOUT
65
SPECIES

Mole crickets live virtually worldwide in suitable damp, grassy habitats.

ADULT LIFESPAN
2
YEARS

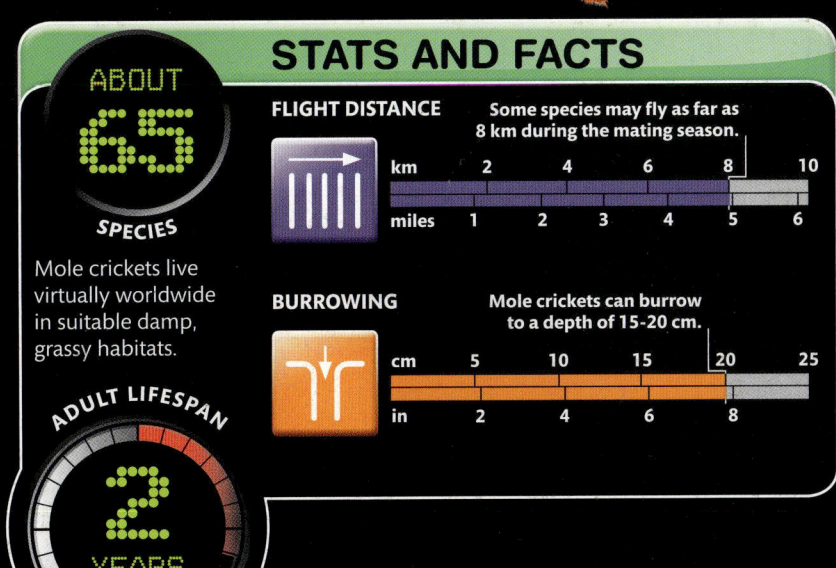

FLIGHT DISTANCE Some species may fly as far as 8 km during the mating season.

km	2	4	6	8	10
miles	1	2	3	4	5	6

BURROWING Mole crickets can burrow to a depth of 15-20 cm.

cm	5	10	15	20	25
in	2	4	6	8	

SPRINTING SPIDER
GIANT HOUSE SPIDER

For some people, the scariest bug is the giant house spider, which invades homes and frightens the occupants by running at high speed across the floor towards them. Males have extra-long legs that allow them to run faster than any other spider. They wander in search of females, which usually stay hidden in their funnel-shaped webs.

Muscles expand and contract the stomach, enabling the spider to suck up liquid food.

Large venom gland

Brain

Spider's eight eyes and other sensory organs are linked to its brain.

VENOMOUS FANGS

Powerful jaws are tipped with sharp, venomous fangs for killing prey. The spider crushes its victims and floods them with digestive saliva. This turns their soft parts to a liquid ready for sucking up.

Big nerves attached to the brain control the spider's eight legs.

Parts of the digestive system extend into the upper leg segments.

STATS AND FACTS

ABOUT
1,200
SPECIES

Fast-running spiders of this type are found worldwide. Many live in houses, but others live in grassy places and scrublands.

 EGGS

The female lays about 60–100 eggs, but only about 2 per cent survive to reach adulthood.

MATING

After mating, the male giant house spider is sometimes eaten by the female.

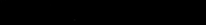 **WEBS**

These spiders spin sheet-like webs in corners of rooms, and wait for prey to get trapped.

SPEED

This speedy spider gets around quick, travelling at about 1.9 km/h (1.2 mph).

APPROXIMATE LIFESPAN
1 YEAR

"This household terror is the fastest thing on eight legs."

- **SIZE** Up to 19 mm (¾ in) long
- **HABITAT** Houses, caves, and rocky places
- **LOCATION** Europe, and introduced to North America
- **DIET** Insects that become trapped in its sheet web

Powerful heart creates the blood pressure that extends to the spider's legs.

Intestine digests the spider's liquified food, and absorbs the nutrients.

CLAWED FEET

Each spider's leg is tipped with a clawed foot, specially adapted for crawling over its web without getting entangled. Sensory hairs detect vibrations and air movements generated by nearby prey.

Spider's book lungs absorb oxygen from the air and get rid of waste carbon dioxide.

Silk glands make the silk that the spider uses to spin its web.

Inside a spider

A giant house spider is typical of the largest group of spiders armed with venomous fangs that nip together like pincers. These fangs and the eight legs are attached to a head-body unit called the cephalothorax, while the abdomen contains the spider's heart and intestine.

The ovary of this female giant house spider produces her eggs.

SILK SPINNERET

The spider's silk is drawn out through the multiple nozzles of the spinnerets on the tip of its abdomen. The size of the nozzles can be altered to control the thickness, strength, and texture of the silk.

ANIMAL ATHLETES

SILK-LINED LAIR

The giant house spider is one of many spiders that live in funnel-shaped webs woven from dense, soft silk. The narrow part of the funnel opens out into a broad sheet that acts as a trap for prey. If an insect stumbles into the web, it sends vibrations through the silk. These alert the spider, which dashes out of its lair to seize its victim, wrap it in a silken shroud, and deliver a venomous, deadly bite.

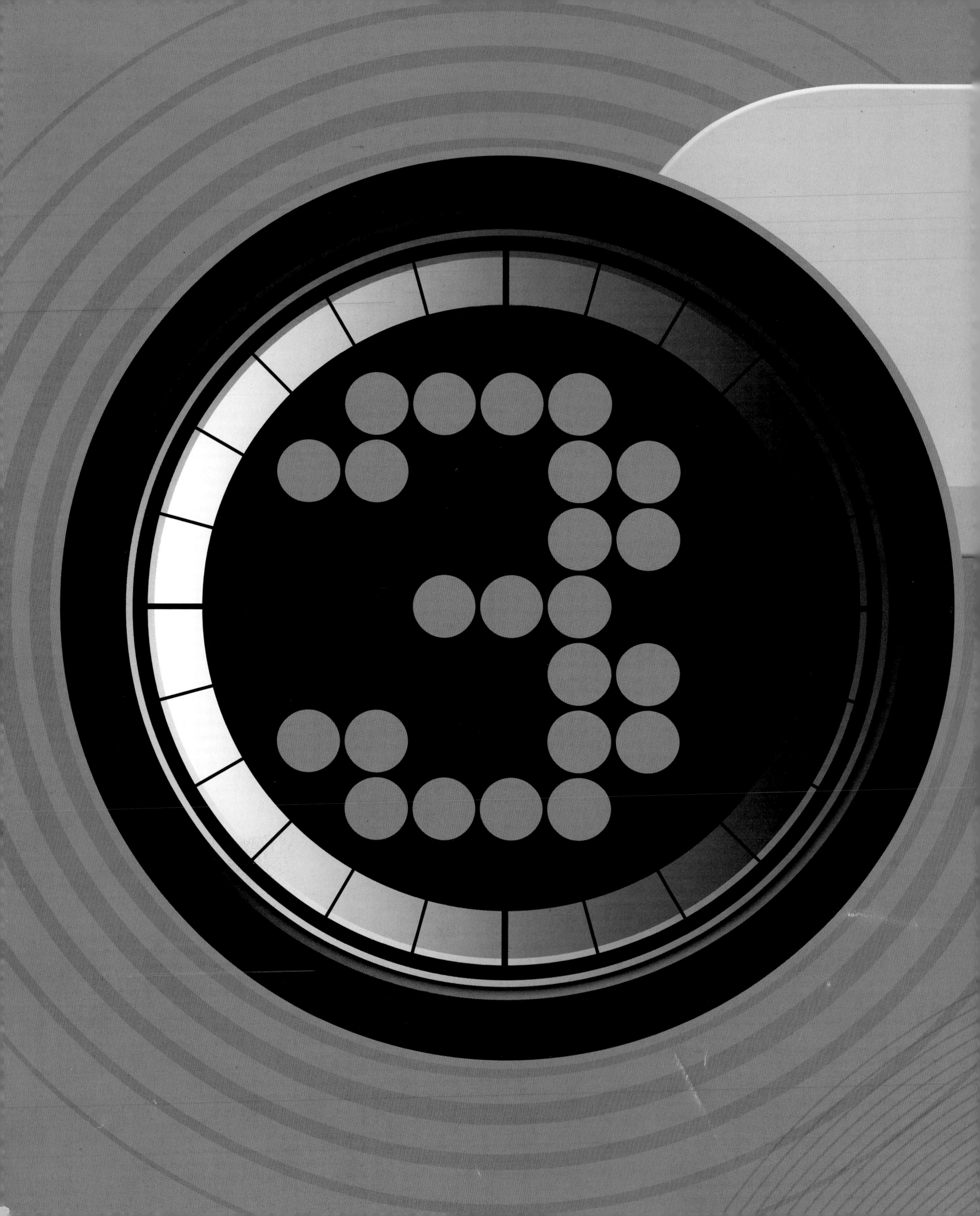

FEARSOME HUNTERS

The undergrowth is teeming with some of the most specialized hunters on the planet. Spiders, scorpions, and assassin bugs are among those armed with deadly weapons for catching and killing prey, while other hunters prefer to eat their victims alive.

PERFECT CATCH

RUFOUS NET-CASTING SPIDER

Many spiders use silk to snare prey, but few are quite so ingenious as the net-casting spider. Like a miniature owl, this night hunter has a huge pair of main eyes for targeting prey in the gloom. It hangs from a simple web near the ground, its four front legs holding a tiny net made from super-stretchy silk. When an insect strays within range, the spider watches and waits, then suddenly extends its legs to stretch the net wide. As the insect touches the net, the spider lets the elastic silk spring back and trap its victim. It is all over in less than a second.

AT A GLANCE

- **SIZE** Up to 2.5 cm (1 in) long
- **HABITAT** Forests, scrublands, and gardens
- **LOCATION** Australia
- **DIET** Ground-living insects and spiders

STATS AND FACTS

ABOUT
48
SPECIES

Net-casting spiders are found across the world in tropical and subtropical regions.

FEMALE LIFESPAN
1
YEAR

EYES

These spiders are also known as ogre-faced spiders because of their huge eyes.

VISION

Eyes have receptor cells that are 200 times more sensitive than spiders that hunt by day.

DEFENCES

The stick-like body enables the spider to blend in with its surroundings.

EGGS

A female spider lays between 100 and 200 eggs in her lifetime.

FULL STRETCH

The net-casting spider's web can be stretched to at least ten times its normal size. When prey becomes entangled by the wool-like silk, there is no hope of escape from the spider's venomous, paralysing bite.

SLIME SHOOTER
VELVET WORM

The insects, spiders, and other bugs with hard external skeletons evolved from an ancient group of animals with soft bodies and flexible legs. Some of these creatures still flourish in moist, warm forests – the velvet worms. Resembling soft-bodied centipedes, these night hunters creep around searching for insects and worms to snare with lassoes of sticky slime.

Ringed antennae are the main sense organs.

Leggy worm

The tiny bumps covering the skin of this multi-legged creature gives the animal its velvet look. Like all velvet worms, this species has many pairs of short, stumpy legs and two fleshy antennae. Nozzles on each side of its head fire a secret weapon – jets of slime.

The slime-squirting nozzles are attached to huge slime glands inside the body.

NIGHT STALKER

Creeping up on its victim in the dark, the velvet worm checks the prey using its antennae. If it likes what it feels, the velvet worm fires two zig-zag streams of sticky slime to trap the prey, before moving in for the kill with a toxic bite.

Bumpy skin is like the flexible skin of a caterpillar, and has no hard parts.

"Velvet worms have **existed** for **570** million years."

GETTING A GRIP

The velvet worm's legs are soft and flexible. They can be bent in any direction by small muscles, but the animal can also move them in pairs by flexing its body. Each leg is tipped with a pair of sharp but retractable claws, which give a good grip on rough surfaces.

The claws are made of hard chitin – the material that forms insect exoskeletons.

AT A GLANCE

- **SIZE** Up to 28 cm (11 in) long
- **HABITAT** Damp places, mainly in forests
- **LOCATION** Central and South America, central and southern Africa, Southeast Asia, Australia, and New Zealand
- **DIET** Ground-living worms, insects, and spiders

STATS AND FACTS

ABOUT
180
SPECIES

Many velvet worms live in the world's tropical forests, but they are also found in cooler climates in the southern hemisphere.

NUMBER OF LEGS   Number of legs varies between 13 and 23 pairs.

0   10   20   30

NUMBER OF YOUNG   Up to 30 per year; some are livebearers; others lay eggs.

0   10   20   30   40

LIFESPAN   UP TO **7** YEARS

ULTIMATE AMBUSH
This robber fly has caught a common whitetail dragonfly – itself a formidable, fast-flying predator. Spearing the victim through a weak point in the armoured body, the fly injects a flesh-dissolving venom.

INSECT ASSASSIN
ROBBER FLY

Most flies are small insects that feed on sugary foods such as flower nectar. But robber flies are aggressive, powerful hunters that attack other insects by ambushing them in flight after targeting them with their big compound eyes. The fiendish fly seizes its victim with strong bristly legs before stabbing it with a sharp beak, injecting a shot of toxic, paralysing saliva. With the onslaught over, digestive enzymes in the saliva liquidize the victim's soft tissues, so the robber fly can enjoy sucking them up like soup.

AT A GLANCE

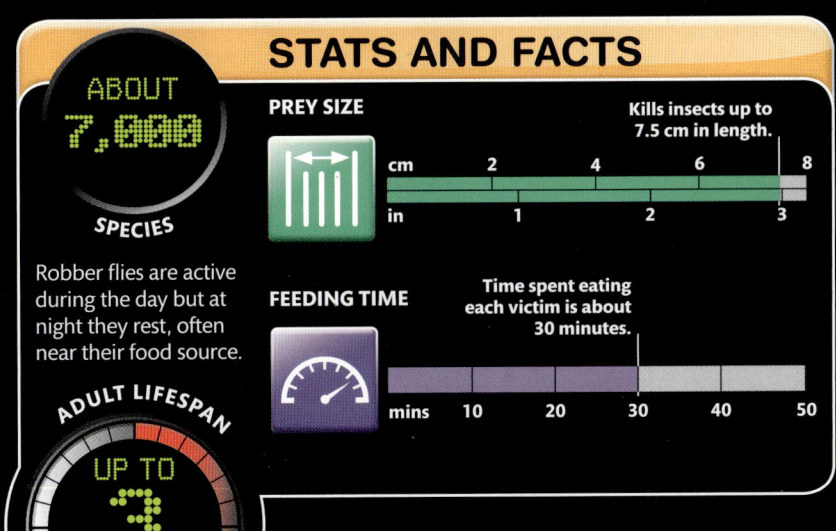

- **SIZE** Up to 5 cm (2 in) long
- **HABITAT** Favours open, hot, and even arid habitats
- **LOCATION** Worldwide
- **DIET** Other insects

STATS AND FACTS

ABOUT 7,000 SPECIES

Robber flies are active during the day but at night they rest, often near their food source.

ADULT LIFESPAN
UP TO 3 MONTHS

PREY SIZE
Kills insects up to 7.5 cm in length.

cm		2		4		6		8
in			1		2		3	

FEEDING TIME
Time spent eating each victim is about 30 minutes.

mins	10	20	30	40	50

A FEAT OF
ENGINEERING

STICKY SPIRAL SNARE
ORB WEB SPIDER

All spiders prey on other creatures, but many do not hunt. They use their silk to weave elaborate traps, and wait for insects and other prey to become entangled. The most spectacular traps are the orb webs of garden and wasp spiders. Stunning spirals of sticky silk are tacked to radiating threads slung between bushes and plants. The spider negotiates its web without trouble, but insects get caught. Their struggles alert the spider, which darts over to wrap its prey in silk and deliver a deadly bite.

AT A GLANCE

- **SIZE** Up to 17 mm (¾ in) long
- **HABITAT** Grassy meadows and hillsides
- **LOCATION** Europe, Asia, and North Africa
- **DIET** Insects such as grasshoppers, flies, and butterflies

STATS AND FACTS

ABOUT 3,000 SPECIES

Found worldwide, the orb weavers make up the third largest family of spiders.

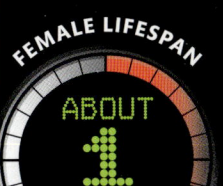

FEMALE LIFESPAN

ABOUT 1 YEAR

RECORD BREAKER

The biggest webs are made by the golden orb web spider. They are 6 m (20 ft) tall and 2 m (7 ft) wide.

TIME

It takes about 60 minutes to build a web, and a spider may have to repair it 2 or 3 times a day.

STRENGTH

Weight for weight, silk strands are 5 times stronger than steel.

SPIDERLINGS

The spiderlings disperse by floating on silk threads, so that they can build their own webs.

PACKED LUNCH

The eyecatching black and yellow wasp spiders often build their webs in long grass to snare the grasshoppers and crickets living there. This spider is wrapping its trapped victim in a shroud of ribbon-like silk, drawn from the spinnerets at the tip of the abdomen.

SILKEN RIBBONS

The webs of wasp spiders and their relatives have zigzag ribbons of gleaming white silk. Scientists are not sure what these are for. One suggestion is that the zigzags – known as stabilimenta – make the web visible to birds, so they do not fly through it and destroy the web. Another theory is that they conceal the spider, making it less likely to be seen and eaten by a predator.

CAMOUFLAGED KILLER

ORCHID MANTID

The spectacular orchids that flower in Asia's tropical forests harbour some deadly secrets. Concealed among the blooms may be an orchid mantid. Its beautiful surface is tinted pink and white and the pretty petal-like plates are a disguise for its legs. Lying motionless, the orchid mantid waits to ambush prey searching for a meal of sweet nectar. When a victim lands within striking range, the mantid seizes the prey with its spiny front legs and eats it alive.

Death trap

An orchid mantid is closely related to the praying mantid, and has the same powerful front limbs. Bristling with spines, these legs work as an automatic trap for prey. The mantid can shoot them out and snap them shut around its victim in a split second, before there is any chance of escape.

STATS AND FACTS

ADULT LIFESPAN
1 YEAR

STRIKE SPEED
The strike speed is less than 100 milliseconds.

DEFENCE
Some mantids use threat displays to scare their enemies.

EGGS
Females lay up to 400 eggs in a protective case.

VISION
The mantid has the ability to turn its head 300°.

ABOUT **2,300**

SPECIES
The orchid mantid is one of a large group of highly predatory insects that are found all over the world in warmer regions.

Large compound eyes have very sharp vision to target insect prey.

The mantid holds its front limbs folded, but ready for instant action.

"A mantid usually eats its prey head first."

SIZE Female up to 7 cm (2¾ in) long; male up to 2.5 cm (1 in) long

HABITAT Tropical rainforest

LOCATION Southeast Asia

DIET Mainly nectar-feeding insects, but will ambush any insect that comes along and even catch small rodents, birds, and lizards

Broad plates on the insect's legs mimic the petals of an orchid flower.

The mantid uses the claws of its four back legs to keep a firm foothold.

The male mantid is much smaller than the female.

RISKY BUSINESS

At less than half the size of the female, a male orchid mantid could be mistaken for a completely different insect. The female is likely to make this mistake, and eat him, so a male in search of a mate must approach with extreme caution – and beat a very quick retreat after mating.

MANTID PARADE

Devil's flower mantid

One of the largest in the mantid family, this east African species lurks on flowers ready to attack. It is disguised to look like shrivelled flower petals, or dried-up leaves.

Dead leaf mantid

Normally, the dead leaf mantid from Asia is almost invisible because it is camouflaged to look like a dead leaf. But when under attack, it rears up in this dramatic display.

Brown mantid

Mantids are fierce predators, but they have their own enemies too. This one uses a terrifying threat display to make it look far more dangerous than it really is, throwing attackers off-guard.

Ghost mantid

The dry and crumpled leaf-like appearance of this small mantid from Africa conceals it among dead leaves. Neither predators nor prey are aware it is there until it is too late.

SINISTER PREDATOR
BEE ASSASSIN BUG

The bee assassin bug certainly lives up to its name. Perched on a flower, the insect waits for a bee to land in search of sweet nectar and pollen. The bee rarely notices the enemy crouching nearby until the bug's powerful front legs take hold. Seizing the victim and probing for a soft spot in the bee's armour, the assassin uses its curved, hollow beak to stab and inject a shot of lethal, flesh-destroying saliva. The fluid digests the soft insides of the bee, turning them to a meaty slush ready for the bug to suck out like soup.

AT A GLANCE

- **SIZE** Up to 3 cm (1¼ in) long
- **HABITAT** Dry areas with flowering plants
- **LOCATION** From the northern USA to as far south as Argentina
- **DIET** Bees and other insects that feed on nectar

STATS AND FACTS

ABOUT 110 SPECIES

Assassin bugs live worldwide, but bee assassins live only in the Americas.

LIFESPAN

3 MONTHS

FEEDING TIME

It takes about 60 minutes for bee assassin bugs to eat (drain) their prey.

mins 10 20 30 40 50 60 70

ACTIVE

Although bee assassin bugs are slow-moving day-time predators, they are good fliers.

WEAPONS

These bugs have sticky forelimbs for grasping prey, as well as venomous saliva.

DEADLY AMBUSH

FATAL ENCOUNTER
Crippled by the paralysing effects of the assassin bug's injection, this pollen-dusted honey bee will soon be sucked dry. When the bug has finished its meal, it tosses the empty husk aside and gets ready to ambush its next victim.

AMBUSH!
This North American trapdoor spider has seized its prey and prepares to strike with its venomous fangs. With its back legs anchored in the burrow, the spider drags the victim down into its hideout.

UNDERGROUND MENACE
TRAPDOOR SPIDER

This stocky spider has a clever trap for catching prey. It lives in a silk-lined burrow that has its own hinged door made of soil and silk. The soil makes the door invisible when closed during the day, protecting the spider from predators. But when night falls, the spider raises the door a little and waits, poised for action with its two front pairs of legs out of the burrow. It can sense the slightest movement of prey. Some trapdoor spiders even lay tripwires around their burrows – any small animal that wanders into the tripwires will be lucky to escape.

AT A GLANCE

- **SIZE** Up to 2.5 cm (1 in) long
- **HABITAT** Mainly open ground, often on sloping banks
- **LOCATION** Southern North America
- **DIET** Insects, other spiders, frogs, small lizards, and mice

STATS AND FACTS

ABOUT 128 SPECIES

Trapdoor spiders live in the warmer parts of the world. Most will stay in the same burrow for their entire lives.

LIFESPAN
ABOUT 5 YEARS

BURROW

The silk-lined burrow can be up to 30 cm deep.

cm	10	20	30
in	4	8	12

SPEED

It takes about 0.3 seconds for a trapdoor spider to strike at prey.

SPIDERLINGS

Each spiderling makes its own little burrow. As it grows bigger, it makes the burrow a bit wider.

LETHAL INVADERS
ICHNEUMON WASP

The nectar-sipping ichneumon wasp looks fragile and harmless, but its offspring are deadly. When a female is ready to lay an egg, she searches for the timber-boring grub of another insect, using her sensitive antennae to detect it deep inside a dead tree. With her long egg-laying tube, she drills down to the grub's burrow, where she lays her egg. On hatching, the wasp larva attacks the grub and slowly eats it alive. By the time the grub dies, the killer is ready to leave the nursery.

POWER DRILL
The ichneumon's egg-laying tube is no broader than a hair, yet it can drill through solid timber. Amazingly, the tube's sharp, swivelling tip is hardened with traces of metal, enabling the wasp to bore through the tough wood fibre.

AT A GLANCE

- **SIZE** Up to 5 cm (2 in) long, plus a very long egg-laying tube (ovipositor)
- **HABITAT** Mainly forests
- **LOCATION** Worldwide
- **DIET** The adult usually sips nectar or plant sap; the larva eats other insect larvae

STATS AND FACTS

ABOUT 24,000 SPECIES

Ichneumon wasps form a huge family of similar insects that live all over the world.

ADULT LIFESPAN
1 MONTH

RECORD BREAKER

cm	5	10	15	20
in	2	4	6	

The giant ichneumon wasp *Megarhyssa atrata* has the longest ovipositor – four times the length of its body.

EGGS
Up to 20 eggs are laid, each with a different grub.

DRILLING
Females of some species take about 1 hour to drill into a grub burrow.

DEADLY EMBRACE
FLOWER SPIDER

For nectar-feeding insects such as bees and hover flies, each visit to a flower could be their last, because lurking among the colourful petals may be a killer – a flower spider. Usually well camouflaged, this tiny hunter sits with its long front legs outstretched, ready to seize an insect and stab it with venomous fangs. On a yellow flower, the spider is almost invisible to its prey, and if it moves on to a white flower, it slowly changes colour to match. Meanwhile, the spider keeps so still that it always catches its victims by surprise.

AT A GLANCE

- **SIZE** Up to 1 cm (over ¼ in) long
- **HABITAT** Mainly yellow or white flowers
- **LOCATION** Europe and North America
- **DIET** Mainly nectar-feeding insects

STATS AND FACTS

ABOUT

42

SPECIES

Flower spiders of various species can be found all over the world.

LIFESPAN

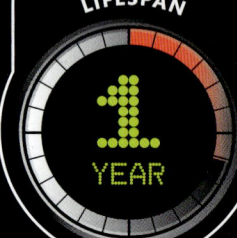

1 YEAR

PREY SIZE

Will take prey up to 2 cm (¾ in) in size, such as honey bees.

DEFENCE

Makes use of camouflage; also hides under a flower, hanging on a thread.

CHANGING COLOUR

It takes about 10–25 days to change from white to yellow, and about 6 days to change to white.

EGGS

A female produces one brood of eggs in her lifetime.

LIQUID LUNCH

With the flower spider's fangs buried in its head, this hover fly was dead within seconds of being caught. The spider injects a venom that liquifies the victim's soft insides, so it can suck up soup for lunch.

FEARLESS HUNTER

HELPLESS VICTIM

Paralysed by the wasp's powerful venom, this tarantula can do nothing to avoid being dragged away to the insect's nursery burrow. The wasp lays a single egg on the spider's motionless body, and fills in the burrow before flying off to find another victim.

TARANTULA TRAPPER
TARANTULA HAWK WASP

Not many insects would choose to tangle with a tarantula, but this giant wasp goes looking for them. Like many wasps it lays eggs on the paralysed bodies of other animals – in this case big, hairy spiders – and when the wasp grubs hatch they eat their victims alive. But first the female wasp must lure a tarantula from its den. The spider is armed with huge fangs, but as it rears up to attack, the wasp curls her tail forward and drives her sting into the tarantula's underside. Within seconds, the spider is helpless, and the wasp claims her prize.

AT A GLANCE

- **SIZE** Up to 7 cm (2¾ in) long
- **HABITAT** Mainly deserts and dry grasslands
- **LOCATION** Southern USA to South America
- **DIET** Adult sips nectar; larva devours a paralysed spider

STATS AND FACTS

ABOUT 18 SPECIES

Spider-hunting wasps live all over the world, but tarantula hawks live only in America.

ADULT LIFESPAN

2–4 MONTHS

PREY SIZE

Up to 10 cm

	cm	5	10	15
	in	2	4	6

DEFENCE
The wasp's vivid colours serve as a warning of its powerful sting.

LARVAE GROWTH
Larvae feast on the spider for 37 days before pupating over the winter.

ALL-ROUND VISION
EMPEROR DRAGONFLY

Big, fast, and vividly coloured, the emperor dragonfly is one of the most spectacular flying insects. It belongs to a family known as hawker dragonflies, which patrol their territory on the wing, watching for airborne prey. The dragonfly can shoot forward, hover, and even fly backwards or sideways to seize flies in its specially adapted legs. This hunter often eats prey in flight, mashing its victim to a pulp with powerful saw-edged jaws.

AT A GLANCE

- **SIZE** About 7.8 cm (3 in) long
- **HABITAT** Over and near ponds, lakes, rivers, and marshes
- **LOCATION** Widespread across Europe, western Asia, and North Africa
- **DIET** Adult eats flying insects; larva eats aquatic animals

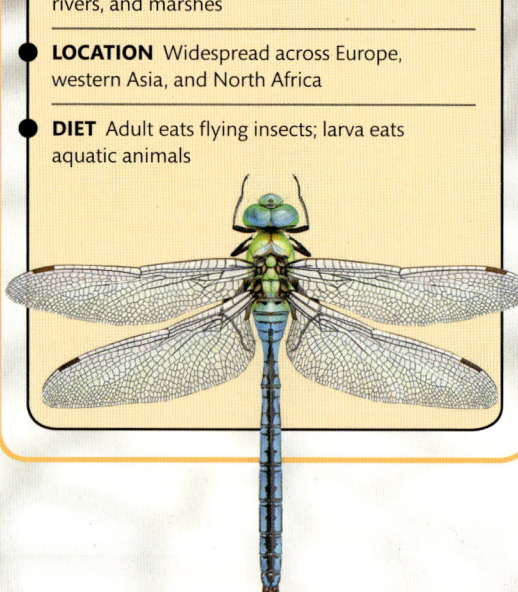

Super vision

A dragonfly hunts by sight using its enormous compound eyes. Each eye is made up of at least 30,000 tiny lenses – five times as many as the similar eyes of a house fly. This gives the dragonfly the sharp vision it needs to both detect its prey and target it with deadly accuracy.

The enormous eyes cover most of the dragonfly's head, giving all-round vision for spotting prey.

STATS AND FACTS

ABOUT 3,000 SPECIES

Dragonflies live all over the world. While some are big hawkers, others are smaller and hunt from perches.

LARVA Larvae live underwater for two years, hunting other insects, tadpoles, and even small fish.

COLOUR VISION A dragonfly may be able to see more colours than a human.

ON TARGET Dragonflies are the world's most efficient hunters, catching more than 95 per cent of their prey.

SPEED Larger dragonflies can fly at speeds of up to 54 km/h (34 mph).

ADULT LIFESPAN UP TO 8 WEEKS

A dragonfly relies more on vision than touch or smell, so its antennae are short.

COMPOUND EYE

The eyes of all adult insects are made up of thousands of cone-shaped units. Each one has its own lens, which focuses light on a cluster of sensory cells. These can only detect a dot of colour, but all the dots add up to create a complete image.

Lens focuses light

Light-sensitive retinal cells

Pigment cells divide one unit from another

The conical units of the dragonfly's eye are packed together like honeycomb cells.

"Insects don't have **eyelids** – they wipe their eyes clean with their forelegs."

JOINING UP THE DOTS

The image created by an insect's compound eye is made up of thousands of coloured dots, like the image formed by the pixels of a digital camera. The more dots there are, the better, and since a dragonfly has more than any other insect, it has the best vision – although we will never know exactly what it sees.

Bristly legs are used for grasping prey and for perching.

AERIAL ACROBAT

A dragonfly's two pairs of long wings are not linked together like the wings of other insects such as butterflies. The dragonfly can move them independently, giving it amazing flight control. It makes the most of this by performing breathtaking aerobatics as it pursues flying prey. This fierce predator is so agile that very few insects can escape it, making it one of the most successful hunters on Earth.

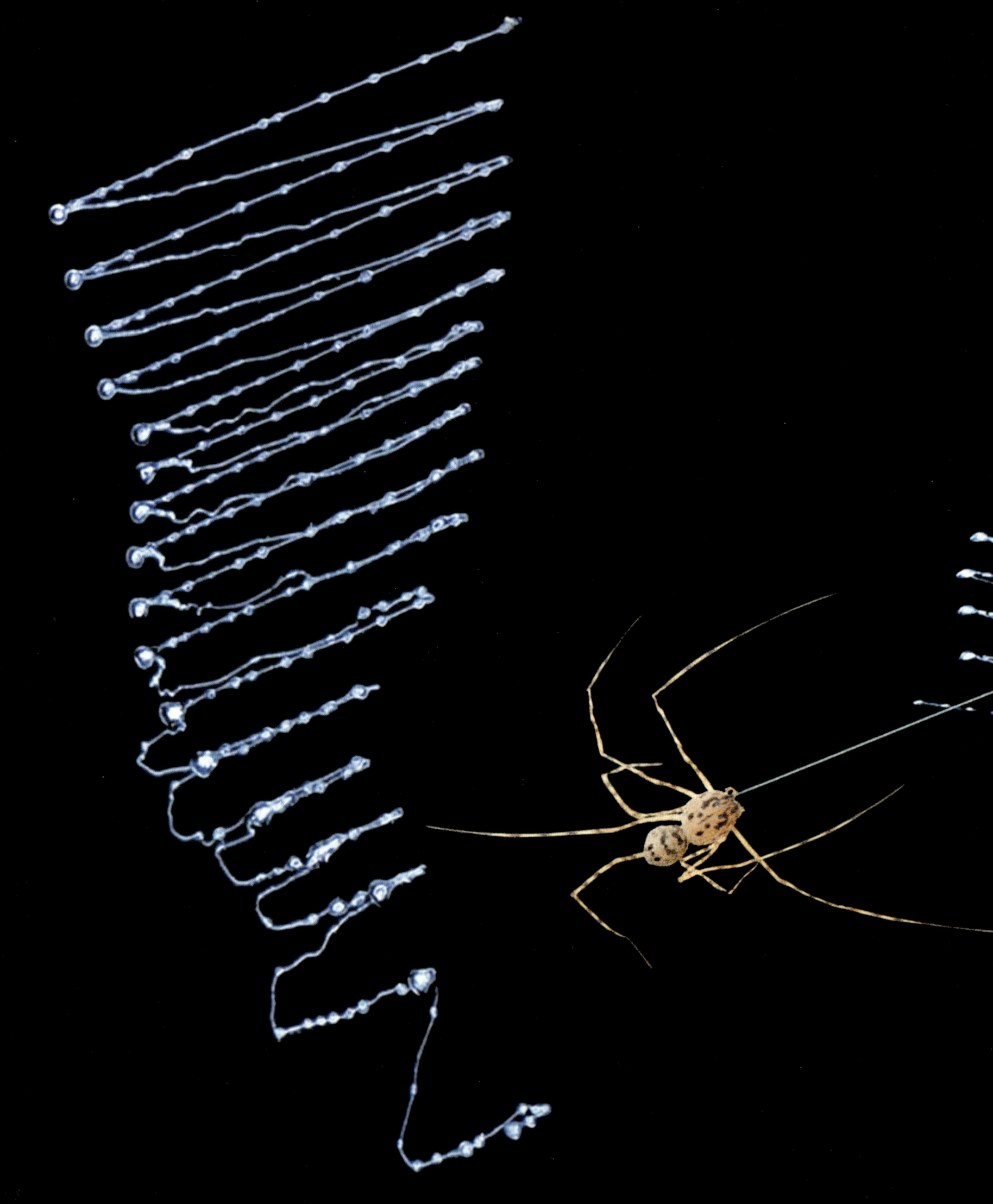

CAUGHT IN THE CROSSFIRE

The spitting spider shoots zig-zags of glue through the air at incredible speed, so there is no time for its prey to escape. The spider shown here has been made to spit its deadly snare on to a glass microscope slide, first with one fang and then the other.

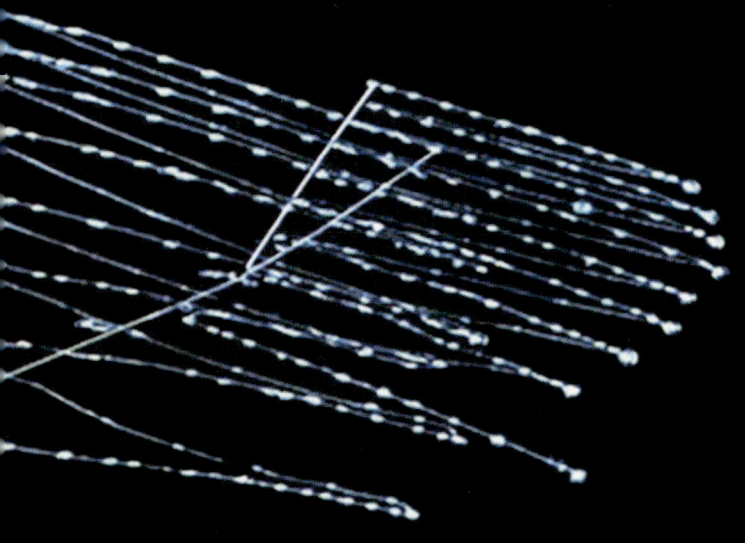

VENOMOUS TRAP
SPITTING SPIDER

This spider looks too tiny to be a threat to anything but the smallest fly, yet it has an extraordinary secret weapon. Its high-domed head contains a pair of enlarged glands that produce venom mixed with a sticky substance that is like liquid silk. When the spider has its prey in sight, it squirts this deadly mixture from its fangs, swinging them rapidly from side to side to create two zig-zag threads of venomous glue. In a split second, its target is pinned down by the poisonous net, and the spider can deliver a final, deadly bite.

AT A GLANCE

- **SIZE** Up to 6 mm (¼ in) long
- **HABITAT** Forests, and often found in houses where the climate is cooler
- **LOCATION** Worldwide
- **DIET** Insects and spiders

STATS AND FACTS

ABOUT 158 SPECIES

The toxic snare is woven by the spider in 1/700th of a second.

LIFESPAN UP TO 3 YEARS

ACTIVE  Usually hunts at night, detecting its prey by sensing air movements.

SPEED  The spider's deadly venom can reach speeds of 28 m/sec (92 ft/sec).

VISION  Most spiders have eight eyes, but the spitting spider has six.

EGGS  Up to 100 eggs are laid by the female spider in cocooned batches of 20–35.

VORACIOUS PREDATOR
GREAT DIVING BEETLE

Beautifully adapted for swimming underwater, the great diving beetle is a ferocious hunter that preys on a variety of aquatic creatures. It uses its long, hair-fringed back legs like oars to drive its streamlined body through the water. The beetle carries a vital supply of air in a bubble beneath its wing cases.

Night flight

Although they spend most of their lives underwater, these beetles can fly very well. They usually take flight at night when they can look for a new pool by observing the light of the Moon reflected in water. But sometimes they land on shiny car roofs by mistake!

COLLECTING AIR

Like all adult insects, the great diving beetle needs to breathe air, so it carries its own supply wherever it goes. The beetle gathers air by swimming to the surface, raising its tail end above the water, and drawing air under its wing cases (elytra). The air supply lasts for several minutes.

The long antennae detect movement and the scent of prey in the water.

Like the exoskeleton, the powerful jaws are made of a tough material called chitin.

Leg-like palps are used to both feel and taste food before it is eaten.

Large compound eyes allow the beetle to see clearly underwater.

Sharp spines help the beetle to seize slippery prey and hold it tight.

STATS AND FACTS

ABOUT
26
SPECIES

Closely related diving beetles live in fresh waters in Europe, Asia, North Africa, and North and Central America.

LARVAL LIFESPAN

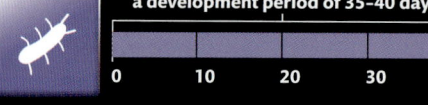

Larvae moult three times in a development period of 35–40 days.

| 0 | 10 | 20 | 30 | 40 | 50 |

BITE

The jaws are strong enough to bite through most prey.

FEEDING

Larvae take about an hour to suck their prey dry.

ADULT LIFESPAN
3 YEARS

Long back legs provide most of the power when swimming.

Females have ridged elytra, but males like this one have smooth elytra.

Air is stored under the elytra.

"A squirt of smelly fluid from its back end keeps enemies at bay."

Fringes of stiff hair on the beetle's legs act like the blades of oars, pushing it through the water.

AMBUSH KILLER

The beetle's aquatic larva is just as ferocious as its parents. Lurking among vegetation or hanging from the surface, it ambushes its prey with long, curved fangs. These inject a flesh-dissolving venom, allowing it to suck its victims dry. The larvae will even prey on each other.

AT A GLANCE

- **SIZE** Adult up to 3.5 cm (1¼ in); larva up to 6 cm (2¼ in) long

- **HABITAT** Freshwater ponds, lakes, and rivers

- **LOCATION** Europe and northern Asia

- **DIET** Aquatic insects, small fish, and tadpoles

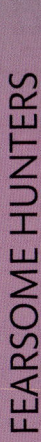

FEARSOME HUNTERS

133

FASTEST-MOVING JAW

FORMIDABLE HUNTER

Jaws locked and ready for action, an Indonesian trap-jaw ant closes in on its target. The slightest touch on one of the jaw's trigger hairs will spring the death-trap and snap it shut.

LETHAL WEAPON

TRAP-JAW ANT

This remarkable ant is armed with one of the most ferociously efficient prey-catching weapons on the planet. When the ant opens wide its jaws, a special mechanism locks them open against the pull of its massive jaw muscles. The mechanism is controlled by whisker-like trigger hairs on the jaws, and when one of the triggers touches anything, it releases the lock. This makes the jaws snap shut at phenomenal speed, seizing the victim and often killing it outright. But the ant also uses its spring-loaded jaw to catapult itself out of harm's way. It does this by snapping its jaws against the ground, launching itself into the air.

AT A GLANCE

- **SIZE** 12 mm (½ in) long
- **HABITAT** Tropical forests
- **LOCATION** Southeast Asia
- **DIET** Insects, spiders, and worms

STATS AND FACTS

ABOUT

70

SPECIES

Trap-jaw ants live in subtropical and tropical regions all over the world.

WORKER LIFESPAN

6

WEEKS

STRIKE SPEED
Jaws snap shut at about 60 meters per second (200 ft per second).

JAW ANGLE
A trap-jaw ant can open its jaws up to an angle of 180°.

COLONY SIZE
Depending on species, the size varies from 100 to 10,000 ants.

DEFENCE
Trap-jaw ants have a sting in their tail, as well as sharp jaws.

NIGHT STALKER
EMPEROR SCORPION

Notorious for their venomous stings, scorpions are relatives of spiders with long, segmented bodies and powerful crab-like pincers. The emperor scorpion is one of the biggest species – an armoured giant that hunts by night in tropical Africa. Almost blind, it stalks its victims by detecting air movements and ground vibrations with special sense organs.

- **SIZE** 20 cm (8 in)
- **HABITAT** Tropical forests and grasslands
- **LOCATION** West Africa
- **DIET** Insects, spiders, lizards, and small mammals such as mice

POWERFUL PINCERS

An emperor scorpion's unusually large pincers are its main weapons. It rarely uses the sting on its tail, relying on sheer strength for killing prey and pulling the body apart. But it may need to sting larger victims like this lizard to stop them struggling.

Sensory hairs on the pincers detect air movements caused by prey.

Small, simple eyes cannot see much but can sense light and shade.

Brain

Massive muscles inside the pincers give a powerful grip.

Sting in the tail

Although it is built like a lobster, the emperor scorpion is a type of arachnid, with many of the same internal features as a spider. But instead of venomous fangs it has a tail sting, and a pair of comb-like sensory organs beneath its body that detect vibrations travelling through the ground.

The last section of the tail contains a pair of venom glands linked to the sting.

The sharp sting can be arched over the scorpion's head to strike prey held in the pincers.

"Scorpions have existed on Earth for 430 million years."

The tail is a slender extension of the scorpion's abdomen, containing part of its intestine.

Main artery pumps a blood-like fluid through the body.

A network of nerve fibres linked to the brain and sense organs controls the scorpion's movements.

One of four pairs of leaved book lungs, which gather oxygen and discard waste carbon dioxide.

Like all arachnids, the scorpion has eight walking legs.

The muscular stomach sucks up fluids; a scorpion cannot swallow solid food.

Salivary gland

DEADLY RELATIVE

The emperor scorpion's sting is no more severe than the sting of a bee, but some other scorpions can kill. The African golden scorpion is one of the most dangerous, with a venom containing a nerve poison that can cause heart failure. It relies on this for hunting, and has relatively small pincers.

EERIE GLOW

If a scorpion is put under a special lamp that produces ultraviolet light – the type of light that causes sunburn – it glows in the dark. This is because its skin contains fluorescent chemicals. Scientists are still not sure how this helps the scorpion.

STATS AND FACTS

ABOUT **1,750**

SPECIES

Scorpions are found throughout the warmer parts of the world, but only 30 of the many species are venomous enough to be dangerous.

ACTIVE
By day, scorpions hide under rocks or in burrows, emerging at night to hunt.

SURVIVAL STRATEGY
Scorpions can slow down their bodies and survive on just one meal a year.

YOUNG
A female scorpion may give birth to as many as 100 live young. She carries them on her back.

DEFENCE
A venomous sting and powerful pincers are used to deter attackers.

LIFESPAN
UP TO **15** YEARS

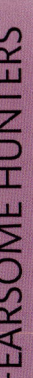

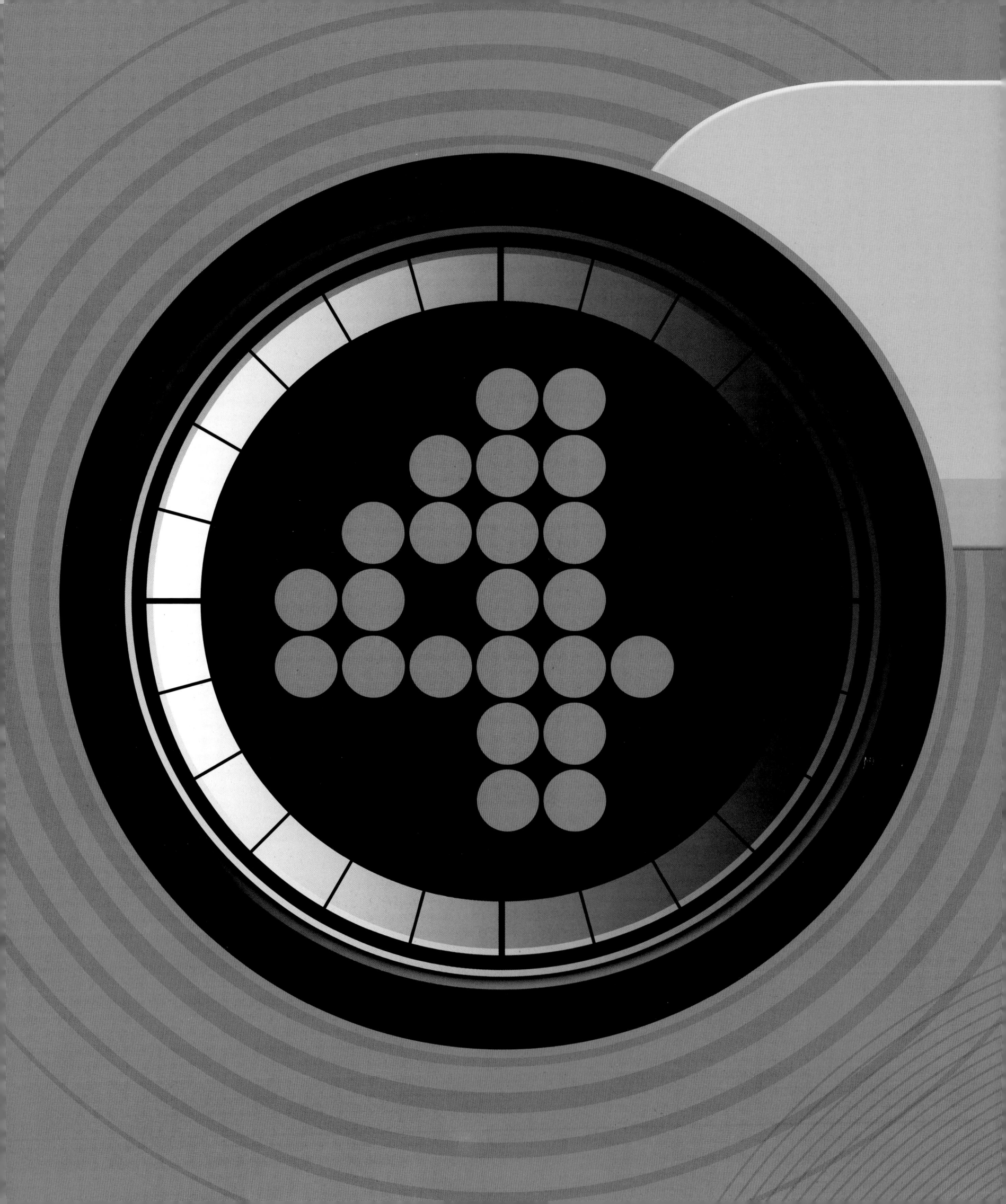

TINY TERRORS

Most bugs give us little trouble, and many are considered to be essential to our survival. But a few are serious pests – they sting, they bite, and they even suck our blood. In doing so, they transmit some of the most deadly of all human diseases.

HOUSEHOLD SCAVENGER
HOUSE FLY

The house fly remains one of the most unpopular insects, and for good reason. Common all over the world, it can carry the micro-organisms that cause more than 100 diseases, including deadly typhoid and polio. The fly picks up the microbes by walking and feeding on human waste, then walking and feeding on the food we eat. In regions with effective sanitation this is not a serious problem, but in places without proper drainage systems any house fly could be carrying a lethal infection.

AT A GLANCE

- **SIZE** About 6 mm (¼ in) long
- **HABITAT** All habitats, but mainly where people live
- **LOCATION** Worldwide
- **DIET** Any type of human or animal food, rotting garbage, and animal faeces

STATS AND FACTS

ABOUT 4,000 SPECIES

One of a family of similar flies, the house fly is the only real threat to humans.

LIFESPAN

UP TO 25 DAYS

EGGS

A female house fly lays about 500 eggs, usually on the food she is eating.

TASTE

A house fly tastes with its feet. These are about 10,000 times more sensitive than our tongues.

HOME RANGE

House flies stay within 3 km (2 miles) of where they were born.

SPEED

These bugs fly at 2 m (6 ft) per second and their wings can beat 200 times a second.

MESSY FEEDER

A house fly feeds by sucking up liquids with spongy, mop-like mouthparts, visible here below its head. It liquefies solid food with a flood of saliva or stomach juice, which may contain disease-causing organisms.

VENOMOUS SPINES
SADDLEBACK CATERPILLAR

Caterpillars are easy targets for hungry birds, which devour them in huge numbers. Many caterpillars protect themselves with irritating bristly hairs, but some take self-defence even further. The saddleback caterpillar has hollow spines capable of injecting an intensely painful venom. Its startling colours serve as a warning to birds, wasps, and other enemies.

Deadly defence
Using their strong, sharp-edged jaws to chew through tough leaves, these saddleback caterpillars spend most of their time eating. Fleshy horns projecting from their vibrant bodies carry the toxic spines that make them dangerous to touch.

"This **caterpillar** is one of the most **dangerous** insects in North America."

AT A GLANCE

- **SIZE** Caterpillar is up to 2 cm (¾ in) long; adult has a wingspan of about 4 cm (1¾ in)
- **HABITAT** Grasslands, woodlands, and gardens
- **LOCATION** Eastern North America
- **DIET** Caterpillar eats leaves of many plants

STATS AND FACTS

ABOUT
1,000
SPECIES

Dangerously spiny caterpillars related to the saddleback are found worldwide, but mainly in warm and tropical countries.

SLUG-LIKE

They are also known as slug caterpillars because of their short, stocky body and the way they glide.

EGGS

Adult female moths lay clusters of 30–50 eggs, and die about three weeks later.

DEFENCE

The saddleback's bright colours warn predators of its toxic spines.

STINGING SPINES

The pain caused by these caterpillars is very similar to the sting of a bee or a wasp.

CATERPILLAR LIFESPAN
UP TO
5
MONTHS

The poison-packed defensive spines pierce skin and often snap off in the wound.

ADULT MOTH

When the caterpillars are fully fed they pupate and turn into stocky brown moths with furry legs. Unlike their younger selves, the moths are harmless. They live just long enough to mate and lay their eggs.

Bright green colouring around the dark "saddle" warns predators to leave it alone.

TOXIC CATERPILLARS

Giant silkworm
The bristles of this South American caterpillar inject a powerful venom that kills about 20 people a year. The venom causes internal bleeding and can lead to brain damage.

Brown-tail moth
Swarms of European brown-tail moth caterpillars feed in trees, protected by silken tents. They have irritating hairs that break off in the skin, causing a painful rash.

Burnet moth
The vivid yellow and black pattern of the burnet moth caterpillar warns birds and other enemies that its body contains cyanide – one of the most deadly poisons.

Puss caterpillar
Despite its cat-like coat, this American caterpillar is far from harmless. The soft fur conceals venomous spines that cause nausea and breathing problems.

BLOODSUCKERS
HARD TICKS

These tiny arachnids are parasites with sharp, piercing mouthparts for sucking the blood of reptiles, birds, and mammals – including humans. They cling on to their victim for several days, drinking up to 500 times their own body weight in blood. In the process, they can transmit nasty viruses, and some of these are deadly if left untreated.

A tick has eight legs, like a spider.

Long wait

Virtually blind, a tick cannot jump or fly, so when it needs a meal it climbs to the tip of a twig or grass stem, and waits. It may wait years for an animal to brush past. Then, sensing the animal's warmth, the tick extends its front legs, clings on, and digs in.

AT A GLANCE

- **SIZE** Up to 1 cm (about ½ in) long
- **HABITAT** Grasslands, moorlands, and forests
- **LOCATION** Worldwide
- **DIET** Blood

BIGGER AND BIGGER

A female tick preparing to breed may feed for eight or nine days, swallowing so much blood that she inflates to ten times her original size. When she can drink no more she pulls out her beak, drops off her host, and lays several thousand eggs. Then she dies.

Swollen with the blood of its victim, this tick is ready to drop off.

STATS AND FACTS

ABOUT 700 SPECIES

Hard ticks have tough, flattened bodies. They cling to plants, waiting for a passing animal to brush past.

BLOOD DIET

A tick needs just three meals of blood in its lifetime.

First meal	Second meal	Third meal
Fuels its change from larva to nymph.	Helps it to change from nymph to adult.	Enables it to breed and lay eggs.

ACTIVE
Ticks mainly search for a victim during the day.

SENSES
Ticks can detect their victims by smell or sensing body heat.

LIFESPAN UP TO 7 YEARS

STEALTH ATTACK

A tick has a barbed beak that it plunges into an animal after puncturing its skin with a pair of serrated pincer-like jaws. The tick uses an anaesthetic to numb the bite, so that the victim does not notice the attack.

MICROSCOPIC RELATIVES

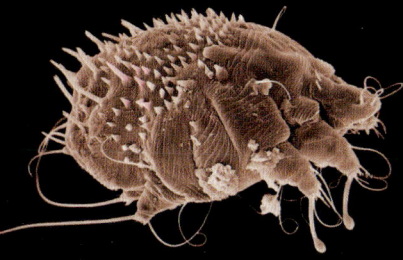

Itch mite

Ticks have tiny relatives called mites. Some of these can also give us trouble, especially the itch mite. This burrows under skin where it feeds and breeds, causing the itching rash called scabies.

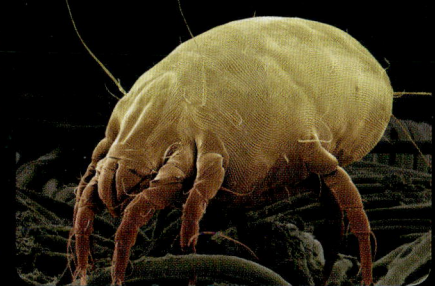

Dust mite

Other mites feed on human skin that has flaked away and settled as dust, so they are called dust mites. They can cause an allergy that makes people sneeze a lot.

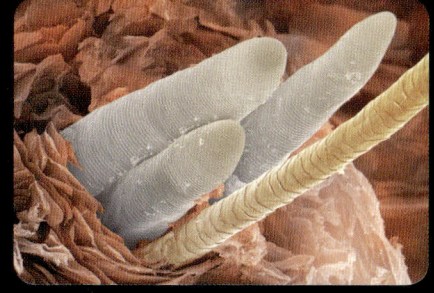

Eyelash mite

Some mites even live in the roots of our eyelashes, though we are unlikely to realize they are there. They feed on skin cells and oils and are a problem only if there are a lot of them, which is unusual.

Beneath the tick's body are plates with tiny holes that allow air into the body.

Before feeding, a tick has a flat body. It may live for years like this.

SPIDER TERROR
SYDNEY FUNNEL-WEB SPIDER

Armed with a potent nerve poison that can kill a person, the Sydney funnel-web leads the list of most dangerous spiders. Related to the giant tarantulas, it has huge fangs that stab downwards like the fangs of a rattlesnake. The female usually stays in her burrow, but the longer-legged male may wander into a garden or house in search of a mate, especially at night when his dark, heavily built body is hard to see.

Deadly defence
In the face of danger, the Sydney funnel-web spider rears up with its front legs in the air, while the long fangs drip deadly venom. If it decides to attack, the spider often clings to its victim and bites multiple times to inject as much venom as possible.

Spurs on the male's second pair of legs grip the female when mating so she cannot bite.

AT A GLANCE

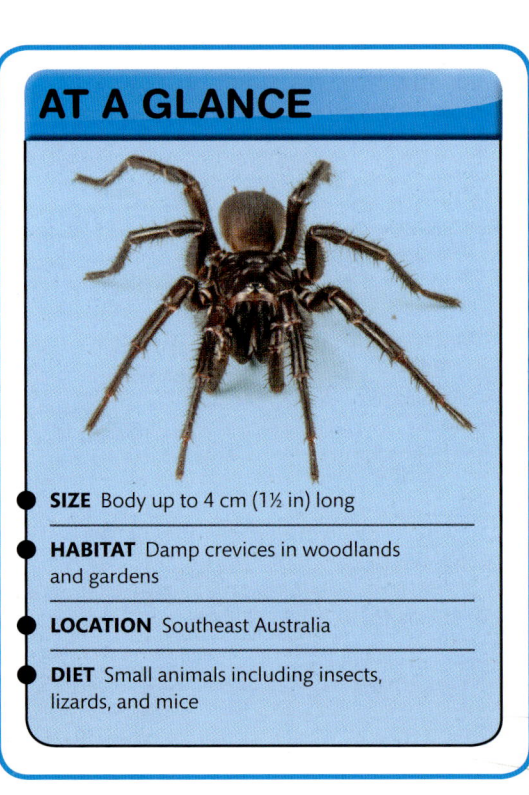

- **SIZE** Body up to 4 cm (1½ in) long
- **HABITAT** Damp crevices in woodlands and gardens
- **LOCATION** Southeast Australia
- **DIET** Small animals including insects, lizards, and mice

STATS AND FACTS

ABOUT
85
SPECIES

This is the most notorious of a group of large spiders that share the same fang structure and make funnel-shaped webs.

EGGS

The female lays about 100 eggs, which are contained in a silken egg-sac inside the spider's burrow.

ACTIVE

These spiders are active mainly at night. During the day, they hide in cool, moist sheltered areas.

DEFENCES
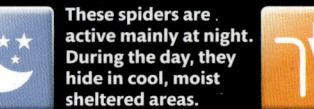
Notorious for its aggressive threat display, this spider's best defence is a venomous bite.

BURROW

The spider's burrow is about 30 cm (12 in) deep and lined with silk. It is often Y-shaped with two entrances.

FEMALE LIFESPAN
UP TO
18
YEARS

DEADLIEST SPIDER

LETHAL VENOM

The venom of a male Sydney funnel-web spider is more potent than that of the female. It attacks the nervous system, causing violent muscle spasms, sweating, sickness, confusion, and eventual heart failure. But there is an antidote, which is made using the venom itself. This has to be "milked" from the fangs of captive spiders by trained – and brave – volunteers.

The male uses his long, specially adapted palps to mate with the female.

Long, sharp fangs are hinged from stout jaws containing the spider's venom glands.

The spider must raise its body to strike because its long fangs point downwards.

KILLER INSTINCT

The risk of being bitten by any spider is very small, but some species are notorious for their powerful venom.

BRAZILIAN WANDERING SPIDER
Big, fast, and aggressive, this species competes with the Sydney funnel-web as the world's most lethal spider. It raises its front legs in the same way to threaten enemies.

BLACK WIDOW SPIDER
Although small, a female black widow spider has large venom glands that produce a powerful nerve poison. Deaths are rare, but the bite is extremely painful.

CHILEAN RECLUSE SPIDER
This is the most dangerous type of recluse spider – a species whose bites create ugly wounds that take months to heal. The venom can also cause lethal kidney failure.

SIX-EYED SAND SPIDER
Found in southern African deserts, this camouflaged spider has the most potent spider venom. Luckily, very few people stumble across it.

DEADLY MENACE
ANOPHELES MOSQUITO

The deadliest bug of all is the mosquito, making other biters and stingers look tame by comparison. This insect carries malaria – a disease that kills more than a million people every year. The microbe that causes the disease lives in the mosquito's body, and is passed on when the insect bites humans to suck their blood.

Long antennae and palps detect the breath of a nearby victim.

Palp

Needle-tipped mouthparts can locate a hidden blood vessel.

The sheath has a sensitive tip that can detect a vein beneath the skin.

Four sharp stylets work together to pierce the skin.

PRECISION TOOL

This close-up shows the mosquito's complex mouthparts. Sharp stylets are protected by a soft, flexible sheath that is pushed up and out of the way when the insect stabs its victim. A slender tube injects saliva to stop the blood clotting, and a broader tube sucks up the blood.

STATS AND FACTS

ABOUT
465
SPECIES

There are thousands of species of mosquito living throughout the world, but only a few tropical species transmit malaria.

ACTIVE
Adults are active at night, with peak activity from midnight to 4 am.

TIMESCALE
Malaria can kill a person in a few days or stay hidden in the body for years.

HEAT TRACKING
Body heat and sweat help mosquitoes to locate their victims.

WINGBEATS
A mosquito's flight muscles beat its wings 400 times a second, making an audible whine.

ADULT LIFESPAN
1-2
WEEKS

Bloodsucking female

Only female mosquitoes suck blood; they need a high-nutrient meal to make their eggs. Humans make ideal victims, because their skin does not have thick fur. A mosquito has long, sharp, tubular mouthparts to pierce the skin, probe for a vein, and suck blood into the insect's stomach.

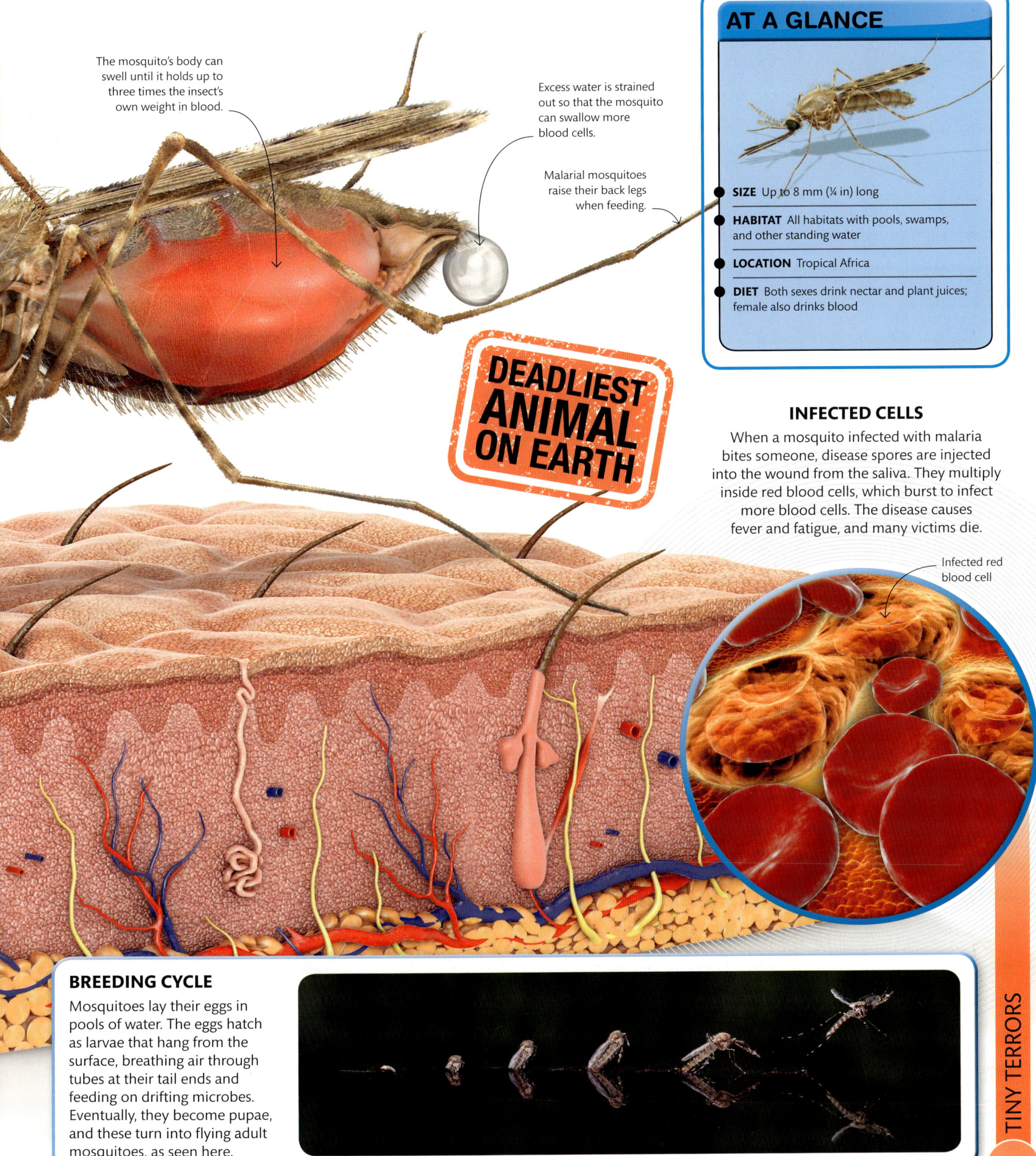

The mosquito's body can swell until it holds up to three times the insect's own weight in blood.

Excess water is strained out so that the mosquito can swallow more blood cells.

Malarial mosquitoes raise their back legs when feeding.

DEADLIEST ANIMAL ON EARTH

INFECTED CELLS

When a mosquito infected with malaria bites someone, disease spores are injected into the wound from the saliva. They multiply inside red blood cells, which burst to infect more blood cells. The disease causes fever and fatigue, and many victims die.

Infected red blood cell

BREEDING CYCLE

Mosquitoes lay their eggs in pools of water. The eggs hatch as larvae that hang from the surface, breathing air through tubes at their tail ends and feeding on drifting microbes. Eventually, they become pupae, and these turn into flying adult mosquitoes, as seen here.

TINY TERRORS

149

KISS OF A KILLER
KISSING BUG

It may be small, but the kissing bug is a killer. It feeds on human blood, creeping up to its victims at night and usually biting them on the face. It has anaesthetic saliva that allows it to feed unnoticed, and when this bloodsucker has drunk its fill, it slips away. But it doesn't just suck blood. Many kissing bugs are infected with Chagas disease – a microbe that attacks muscle and nerve cells all around the human body and causes a violent fever. It can lead to heart failure, and some sufferers die within a few weeks of infection.

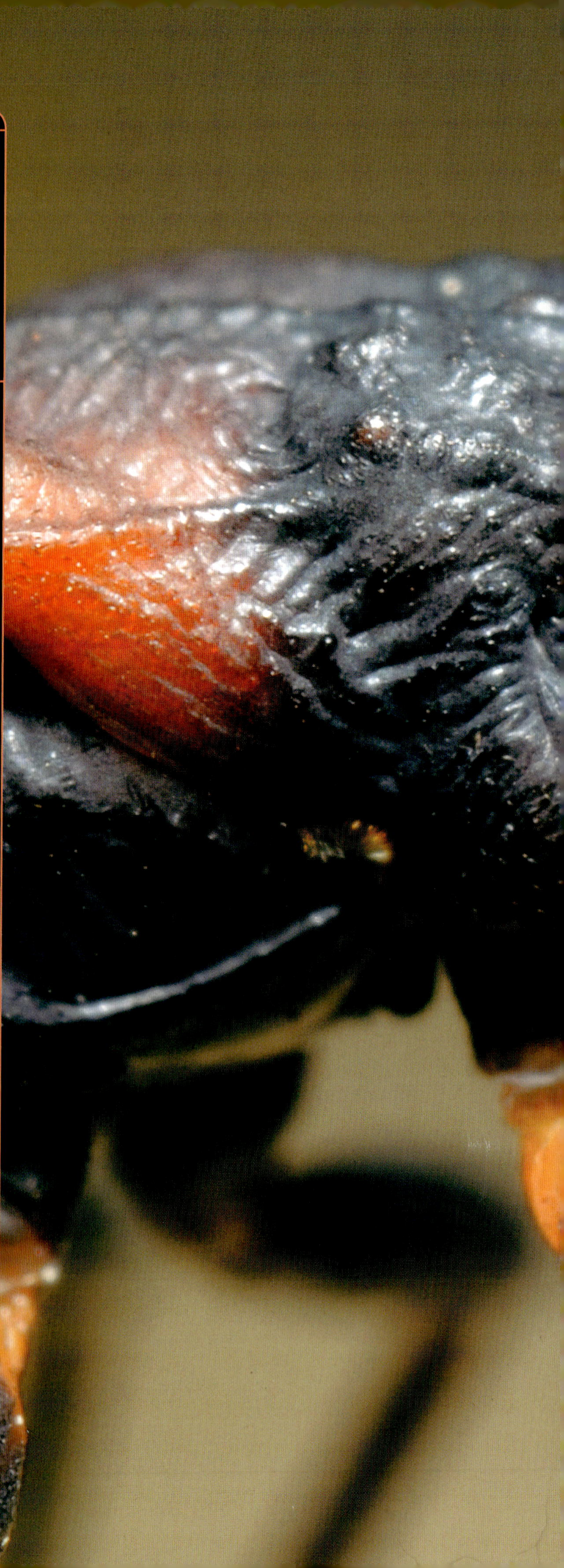

AT A GLANCE

- **SIZE** Up to 2 cm (¾ in) long
- **HABITAT** Forests, grasslands, and houses
- **LOCATION** Tropical South America
- **DIET** Blood

STATS AND FACTS

ABOUT
78
SPECIES

Although the most dangerous kissing bug is tropical, similar ones live in North America.

LIFESPAN

UP TO **12** MONTHS

EGGS

Between 100 and 600 eggs are laid by a female during her 3–12 month lifespan.

DEFENCE

They produce a nasty smell or make a squeaking sound to deter a predator.

TARGETING PREY

Attracted to body heat, the bugs feed on pets as well as people.

LIQUID DIET

After feeding, the bug swells up to four times its weight in blood.

PERFECT PROBE
The kissing bug is a relative of the assassin bugs – murderous insects that inject their victims with flesh-destroying saliva and then suck them dry. Their mouthparts are sharp, hollow needles, ideal for the job in hand.

UNINVITED GUESTS
COCKROACHES

The first cockroaches appeared on Earth more than 300 million years ago, and they have been hugely successful ever since. These bugs can eat virtually anything, and thrive almost anywhere – from hot deserts to Arctic tundra. Notoriously, a few species flourish in houses, feasting on our food at night and slipping out of sight by day.

Unfussy eaters

The German cockroach probably originated in Southeast Asia, but its love of living in warm buildings has allowed it to spread around the world. This scavenger eats any human food available, fouling it with excrement in the process. When food is scarce, the cockroaches resort to nibbling on soap, glue, or even each other.

Front part of the body is protected by a strong shield called the pronotum.

The front wings are tough and leathery.

AT A GLANCE

- **SIZE** Up to 16 mm (⅝ in) long
- **HABITAT** Mainly buildings where food is prepared
- **LOCATION** Worldwide
- **DIET** Prefers to eat meaty, starchy, and sugary foods

STATS AND FACTS

ABOUT 4,500 SPECIES

Thousands of species of cockroach are found worldwide, but only about 30 of them live in buildings and are considered pests.

ROBUST BUGS

Some species are among the hardiest insects, surviving for several weeks on very little food.

EGGS

A female German cockroach produces about five egg cases. These contain about 40 eggs each.

GROWTH

A cockroach sheds its skin about six times before reaching adult size.

RECORD BREAKER
Weighing about 35 g (1 oz), the giant cave cockroach from Central America is the heaviest cockroach in the world.

GERMAN COCKROACH LIFESPAN

3 MONTHS

OTHER COCKROACHES

Although cockroaches are considered a nuisance, most species never cause any trouble. They live in forests, grasslands, swamps, caves, and other wild habitats, where they feed on a range of animal and plant material. They are an important part of the food chain, recycling waste matter and returning essential plant nutrients to the soil.

Giant cockroach

At up to 10 cm (4 in) long, the giant cockroach deserves its name. It lives in tropical American forests, usually settling in hollow trees and caves.

Hissing cockroach

Native to Madagascar, this large, wingless cockroach lives in decaying timber. It makes a hissing sound by forcing air out of its spiracles.

Dried leaf cockroach

This Southeast Asian forest cockroach is one of many species that look after their young. The cockroach nymphs are wingless miniatures of the adults.

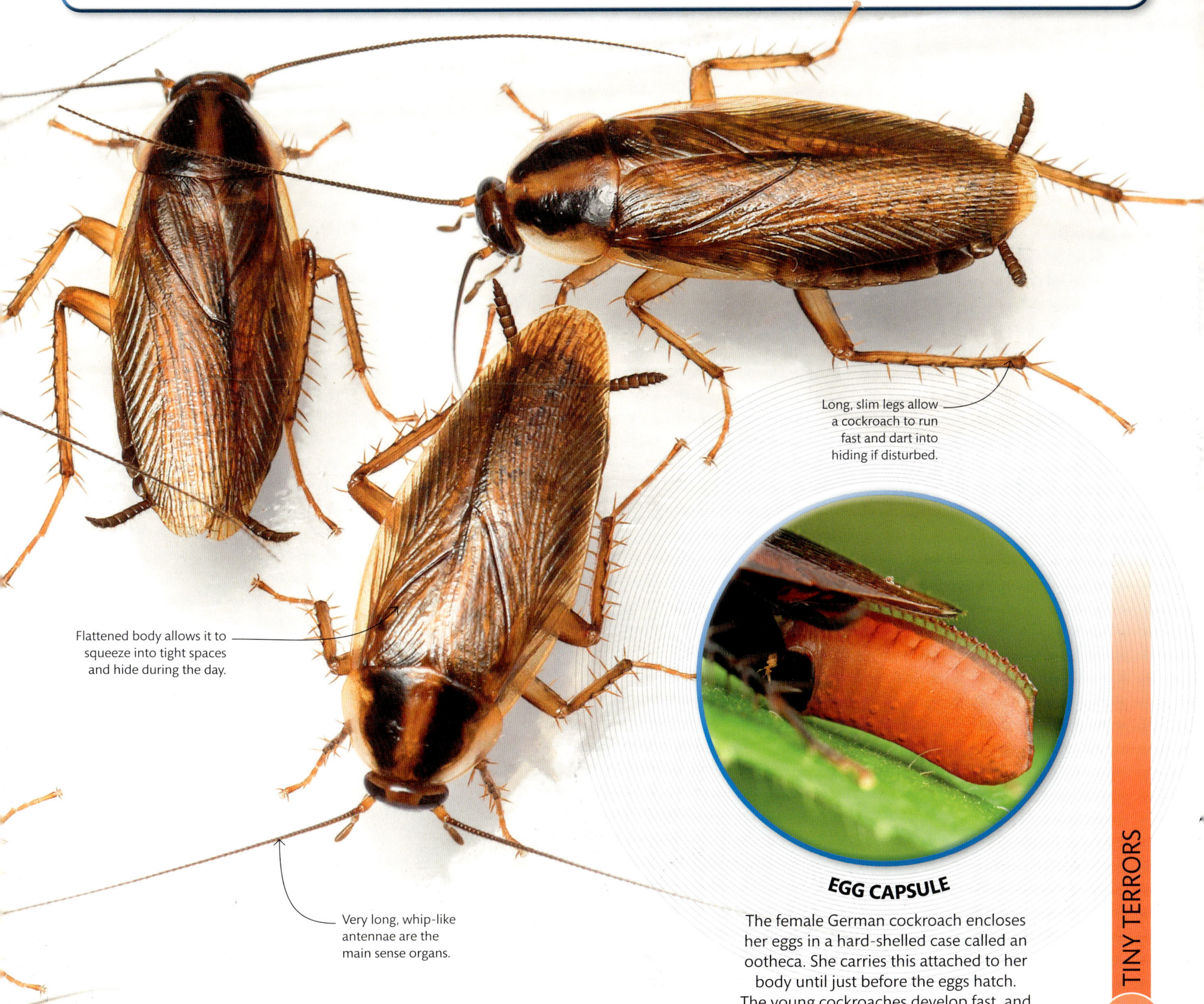

Long, slim legs allow a cockroach to run fast and dart into hiding if disturbed.

Flattened body allows it to squeeze into tight spaces and hide during the day.

Very long, whip-like antennae are the main sense organs.

EGG CAPSULE

The female German cockroach encloses her eggs in a hard-shelled case called an ootheca. She carries this attached to her body until just before the eggs hatch. The young cockroaches develop fast, and are ready to start breeding within 60 days.

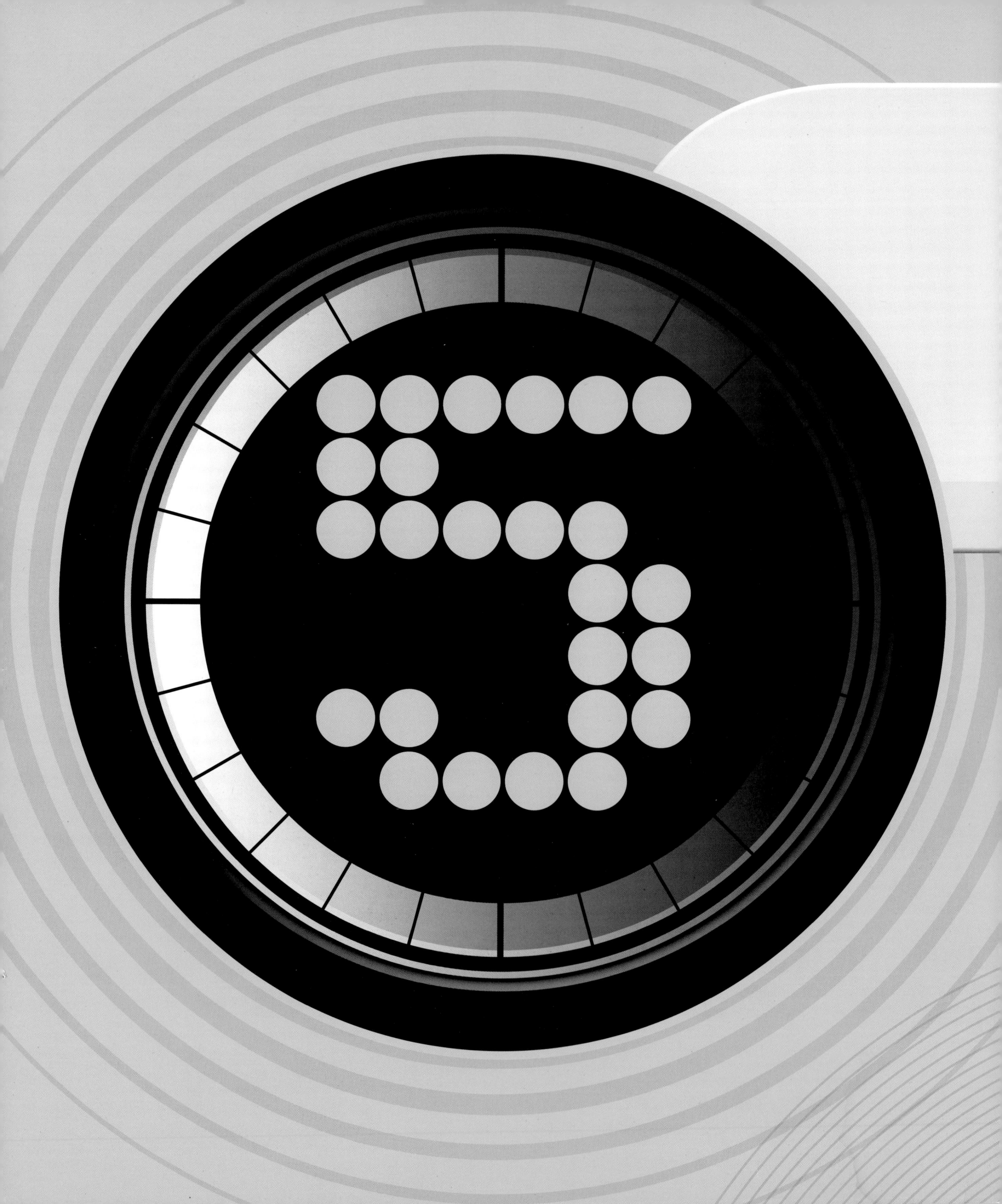

LIFE STORIES

Many bugs lead extraordinary lives. Some live in vast colonies and cannot survive alone, while others spend part of their lives in completely different bodies. Several species have jaw-dropping ways to raise their young, and a few can even survive being frozen solid.

RED ALERT
RUBY-TAILED WASP

This jewel-like insect may shine bright, but the brilliance hides a dark side. The wasp is a nest parasite, like a cuckoo, and is often called a cuckoo wasp. It slips into the nest of a solitary wasp or bee and lays an egg. When the egg hatches, the larva eats the young of the nest owner.

BALL OF DEFENCE

Invading the nest of a wasp or bee is dangerous, because its owner is armed with a deadly sting. But the cuckoo wasp defends itself by curling into a tight ball. The thick chitin of its back and tail acts as an effective sting-proof armour.

Dazzling display

Some of the striking colours of the ruby-tailed wasp are created by light reflected from its body. Tiny bumps and dimples on the shiny external skeleton scatter the light and create a rainbow effect called iridescence. This changes with the angle and strength of the light, and the wasp is always at its most dazzling in strong, direct sunlight.

Like most wasps, this insect has two pairs of transparent wings.

Armoured abdomen has a hollow-shaped underside, where the wasp tucks its legs when curled up.

Female wasp has a strong egg-laying tube (ovipositor).

Even the legs glitter with rainbow colours in bright sunlight.

AT A GLANCE

- **SIZE** Up to 12 mm (½ in) long
- **HABITAT** Mainly dry places
- **LOCATION** Worldwide
- **DIET** Adults eat nectar and pollen; young eat larvae of wasps and bees

RISKY STRATEGY

Some of the cuckoo wasp's main targets are solitary bees that nest in cavities or burrows in the ground. This bug must slip into the nest and lay an egg without being noticed by the parent bee, so it watches and waits for the bee to fly off before making a move. The cuckoo wasp must work fast before the bee returns, although it can defend itself when threatened.

This ruby-tailed wasp waits at the nest entrance for a bee to leave.

Big, bulging compound eyes help the wasp target its victims.

Sensitive antennae curve down to detect the scent of a nest burrow.

STING-PROOF ARMOUR

STATS AND FACTS

ABOUT **1,000** SPECIES

Cuckoo wasps of different species are found in habitats all over the planet. They share the same habits, and most are brightly coloured.

ACTIVE
These solitary wasps are very active during the day, running over walls and tree trunks looking for hosts.

YOUNG
Larvae complete their growth in the host insect's nest, and emerge the following year.

COLOUR
Various species all look similar with their shiny jewel-like colours of blue, red, green, and bronze.

STING
Although these wasps have a sting, it is not functional as most species do not have venom.

ADULT LIFESPAN UP TO **3** MONTHS

BURYING BEETLE

SEXTON BEETLE

The ground would be littered with small dead animals if it were not for insects like the sexton beetle, which uses them as food for its young. Attracted by the scent of decay, a pair of male and female beetles dig beneath the body so that it sinks into the ground. If the earth is too hard, they drag the corpse to a more suitable spot. Once the body is buried, the female lays her eggs on it. When the larvae hatch, they feed on the meat until they are ready to turn into adult beetles. Meanwhile, their mother keeps her young safe from enemies and even feeds them.

AT A GLANCE

- **SIZE** Up to 2 cm (¾ in) long
- **HABITAT** Grassland and woodland
- **LOCATION** Europe, northern Asia, and North America
- **DIET** Dead animals

STATS AND FACTS

ABOUT
150
SPECIES

Similar burying beetles are foumd throughout the world. They all share the same taste for carrion.

LIFESPAN
UP TO
1
YEAR

SMELL

Sexton beetles can smell a dead animal up to 1.6 km away.

| km | 0.5 | 1 | 1.5 | 2 |
| miles | | ½ | 1 | |

STRENGTH

Two sexton beetles can move a dead rat weighing 450 g (1 lb).

ACTIVE

Sexton beetles are mostly active at night, and bury their find immediately.

BODY DETECTOR

Sexton beetles have incredibly sensitive antennae that can detect a dead mouse from an astonishing distance. Sometimes, five or six beetles land on the same corpse, but the first pair to arrive usually drive off any competitors.

NATURE'S RECYCLERS
DUNG BEETLE

The dung of cattle and other grazing animals might look and smell disgusting to us, but to dung beetles it is a rich source of nutrients. They use it as food for their young, burying the dung beneath the ground and laying their eggs within it. In the process, the beetles recycle vast amounts of animal waste, adding to the soil's fertility.

Tunnellers

Some dung beetles, such as these European dor beetles, burrow deep beneath piles of horse or cattle dung. The females stock the end of each tunnel with a pellet of dung before laying an egg inside it. Then they seal the tunnel with soil.

Dor beetles smell fresh dung from long distances, so many fly in from all directions.

The ground beneath a cowpat is dug out before the beetles start removing and burying the dung.

DIGGING DEEP

Dor beetles use their strong front legs to dig a network of tunnels beneath the dung. The legs have tooth-like projections that help to dig away the soil.

Deeper parts of the burrows are dug first; side passages are filled in after the eggs are laid.

The size of each dung pellet is perfectly measured to provide a year's food supply.

BURROWS
The burrows dug by tunnelling beetles can reach depths of up to 50 cm (20 in).

ACTIVE
Studies show that nocturnal dung beetles use the night sky to help them navigate.

EGGS
A female beetle lays between 3 and 20 eggs at one time.

WEIGHT
In one night, a dung beetle can bury 250 times its own body weight of dung.

SPECIES
MORE THAN 5,000

Different species of dung beetle live all over the world, feasting on the dung of the native animals.

ROLLERS AND DWELLERS

Some species of dung beetles work hard to roll balls of dung away from the dung pile, while others lay their eggs within the pile itself.

ON A ROLL
These dung beetles create balls of dung by rolling them over the ground. Each ball can be 50 times the weight of the beetle, and is buried as food for the young.

ON TOP OF THE PILE
Rather than use energy rolling dung balls or digging deep burrows, dweller beetles tunnel into the dung pile and use it as an edible nursery for their larvae.

BEETLE GRUB

When the beetle grub hatches, it feeds on the buried dung pellet for a year. The dung provides its entire food supply. As the grub grows, it sheds its soft skin several times before becoming a pupa – the phase of life when the insect changes into an adult beetle.

ANTIFREEZE
BEETLE

SUPERCOOL SURVIVOR
RED FLAT BARK BEETLE

Warm-blooded animals can survive freezing weather because they turn food energy into heat. Bugs cannot do this, so they risk being killed by ice crystals growing in their body tissues and destroying them. The American red flat bark beetle combats this with natural antifreezes in its blood, which protect it through the bitter Alaskan winter. Amazingly, the beetle can freeze solid like glass as it lies dormant beneath the bark of fallen trees, but still survives because the concentrated antifreezes stop the formation of the crystals that do the damage.

AT A GLANCE

- **SIZE** Up to 14 mm (½ in) long
- **HABITAT** Forest trees
- **LOCATION** Northwestern North America
- **DIET** Insects

STATS AND FACTS

14
SPECIES

Different species of flat bark beetle live in all the northern forests of the world.

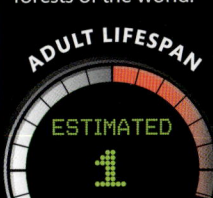
ADULT LIFESPAN
ESTIMATED
1
YEAR

TEMPERATURE

 These beetles can survive temperatures as low as -150°C (-238°F).

COLOUR

Depending on species, flat bark beetles are also brown or yellow.

LIFE CYCLE

The larval stage lasts for 2 years. The larvae can also survive extreme temperatures.

years	1	2	3

Pupa to emerging adult takes 2 weeks.

IN A TIGHT SPACE

In summer, the red flat bark beetle hunts other insects beneath loose tree bark, making the most of its flattened shape to slip into the tightest crevices. It can even attack insects that have bored tunnels deep into the timber.

SUPREME BUILDERS
TERMITES

Few animals can rival the termites for architectural skill. These mostly tiny, blind insects live in huge colonies. They build complex nests in mounds of hardened mud that often tower over the surrounding landscape. The nests of some species contain special areas used for growing their food, and are cooled by cleverly engineered air-conditioning systems.

Tunnels allow the termites out of the nest to gather supplies.

SUPER STRUCTURES

There are many types of termite mound that display amazing engineering. In hot, dry northern Australia, compass termites build wedge-shaped mounds with the sharp edge facing north. This allows the morning and evening Sun to warm the broad sides of the nest, but reduces the area facing the Sun during the hottest part of the day.

Termite mound
The tall mounds of African savanna termites conceal chambers containing the breeding queen, her developing young, and the fungus gardens that the termites rely on for food. Heat generated from the colony is carried away by air rising to the top of the mound, which can reach up to 7.5 m (25 ft) high.

EMERGENCY REPAIRS

If the colony's nest is broken into, hundreds of worker termites rush to rebuild it. They carry mouthfuls of soil and waste, which they plaster in place to repair the damage. Meanwhile, heavily armed soldier termites stand by to defend the workers and attack any intruders.

STATS AND FACTS

MORE THAN
3,100
SPECIES

The termites that cultivate fungus gardens are one of many different groups of termites that live in the warm parts of the world.

EGGS

The queen may lay up to 30,000 eggs a day, which is one every three seconds.

DEFENCES

Soldier termites can bite, squirt toxic glue, or even burst their bodies to cover attackers in slime.

COLONY

A colony may consist of up to 7 million termites.

WEIGHT
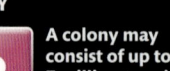
The total weight of termites on the African savannas is twice the weight of all the big animals living there.

QUEEN'S LIFESPAN
UP TO 15 YEARS

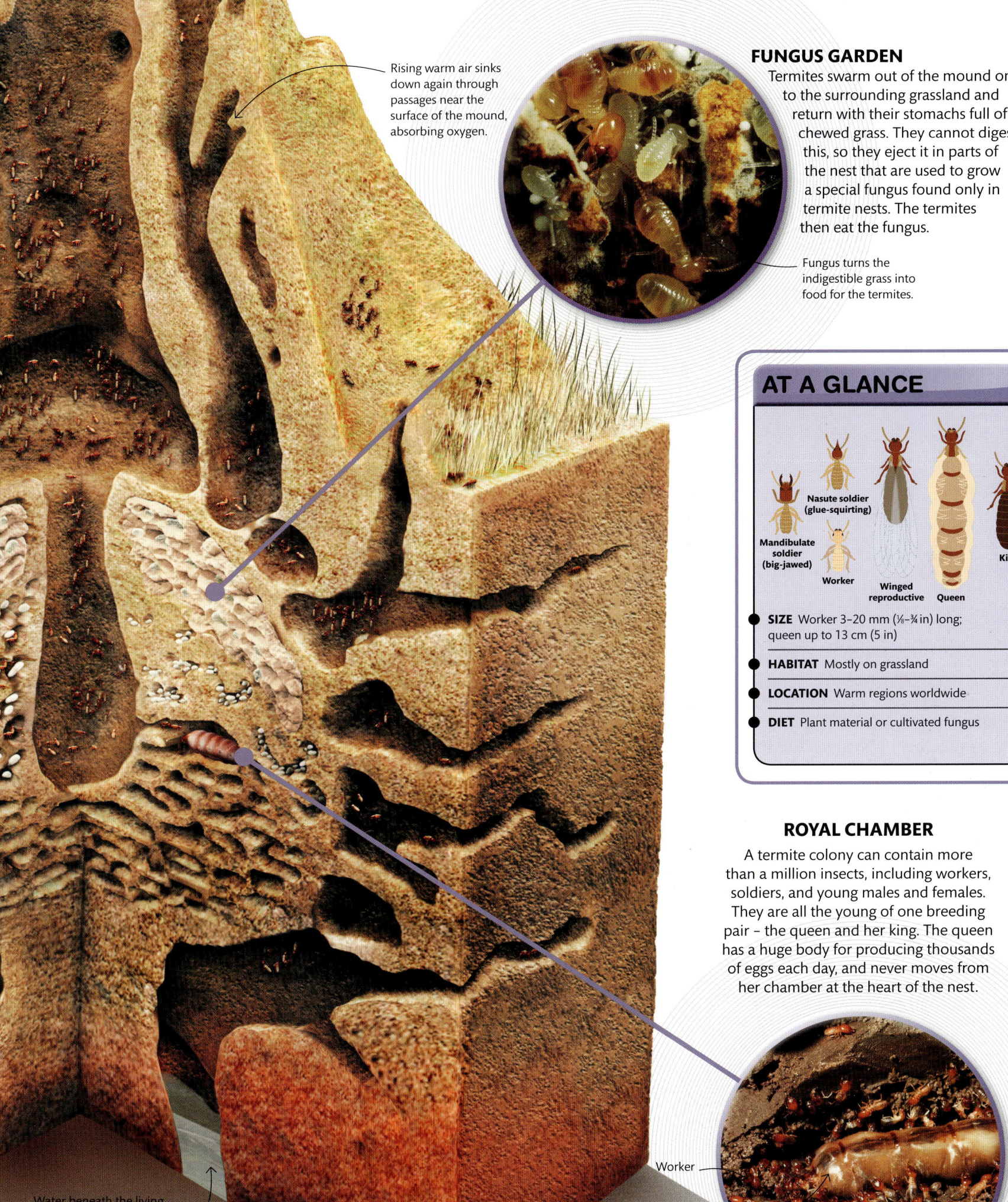

Rising warm air sinks down again through passages near the surface of the mound, absorbing oxygen.

FUNGUS GARDEN

Termites swarm out of the mound on to the surrounding grassland and return with their stomachs full of chewed grass. They cannot digest this, so they eject it in parts of the nest that are used to grow a special fungus found only in termite nests. The termites then eat the fungus.

Fungus turns the indigestible grass into food for the termites.

AT A GLANCE

Mandibulate soldier (big-jawed)

Nasute soldier (glue-squirting)

Worker

Winged reproductive

Queen

King

- **SIZE** Worker 3–20 mm (⅛–¾ in) long; queen up to 13 cm (5 in)
- **HABITAT** Mostly on grassland
- **LOCATION** Warm regions worldwide
- **DIET** Plant material or cultivated fungus

ROYAL CHAMBER

A termite colony can contain more than a million insects, including workers, soldiers, and young males and females. They are all the young of one breeding pair – the queen and her king. The queen has a huge body for producing thousands of eggs each day, and never moves from her chamber at the heart of the nest.

Water beneath the living area moistens the air flowing through the nest.

Worker

Queen

GLUE GUNS

Termite colonies are defended by soldiers – workers that are specialized for attacking their enemies. The soldiers of most species have big, sharp, powerful jaws, but one group of termites has evolved a different weapon. The heads of the soldiers have long snouts that squirt sticky, slightly toxic chemicals. These are especially effective at deterring ants, which are the main enemies of termites.

PRODUCTION LINE
PEA APHIDS

Many insects multiply at an astonishing rate when they have plenty of food. The champion breeders are aphids – small bugs that suck the sweet sap of plants. The pea aphid feeds on pea plants and their relatives. When these are growing well in summer, the aphids breed as fast as possible. Without mating, the females give birth to a stream of females that within days are able to breed in their turn. As summer ends, the aphids produce both females and males. These mate and lay eggs that survive the winter to hatch into more aphids in spring.

AT A GLANCE

- **SIZE** Up to 4 mm (⅛ in) long
- **HABITAT** Woodland, grassland, farmland, and gardens
- **LOCATION** Almost worldwide, wherever its food plants grow
- **DIET** Sugary sap of plants belonging to the pea family

STATS AND FACTS

ABOUT
4,400
SPECIES
Thousands of aphid species live all over the world. Many are able to breed fast without mating.

LIFESPAN
UP TO
40
DAYS

DEFENCE Aphids can kick with their hind feet. Some send out chemical alarm signals.

COLOUR Although mostly green, some aphid species can be pink, black, brown, or even colourless.

YOUNG Within just a month, a female could have a million descendants.

HELPING ANTS Some ants protect aphids in order to feed on the sugary liquid they release.

PERFECT COPY
This pea aphid is giving birth to a miniature version of herself, which will soon be able to have its own young. But because the new aphid has no father, it is an exact clone of its mother.

"A female aphid produces up to 12 young every day of her life."

BUSY BEES
HONEY BEE

No insect is as important to humanity as the honey bee. Valued for thousands of years as a honey producer, the honey bee performs a super service for farmers, pollinating plants that are grown for food. It lives in big colonies, ruled by a single queen who lays all the eggs. The other honey bees are her daughters and sons.

Bees have two pairs of wings. These are joined together by tiny hooks so that the wings can move as one.

MAKING HONEY

Foraging honey bees return to their nest or beehive with their crops full of sugary nectar. They pass this to other bees, who add enzymes that change its chemical nature. Placing the sweet nectar in wax honeycomb cells, the bees then use their wings to fan it, removing most of the water. This stored honey feeds the colony throughout winter.

A worker bee has a sharp, barbed sting, used to defend the colony.

The bee has a pad of bristles on each back leg, which it loads with pollen. They are called pollen baskets.

Hair covering the body traps pollen when the bee visits a flower to feed.

AT A GLANCE

- **SIZE** Up to 2 cm (¾ in) long
- **HABITAT** Forests, grassland, farmland, and gardens
- **LOCATION** Originally eastern Asia, but introduced almost worldwide
- **DIET** Adult drinks nectar; young are fed on honey and pollen

Strong lower leg segment is used to compress pollen into pellets.

Vital service

Honey bees make their honey from nectar that they gather from flowers. In the process, they are dusted with pollen, which needs to be transferred to other flowers to fertilize their seeds. These insects do the job perfectly. They also collect some pollen for their young to eat.

STATS AND FACTS

7
SPECIES

There are thousands of bee species, but only a few of them make enough honey to be known as honey bees.

COLONY

There can be up to 80,000 honey bees in a colony.

| 0 | 20,000 | 40,000 | 60,000 | 80,000 | 100,000 |

EGGS

The queen honey bee lays up to 2,000 eggs every day. Most will develop into female worker bees.

HONEY

About 10 million trips are made by worker honey bees to produce 450 g (1 lb) of honey.

QUEEN BEE LIFESPAN

UP TO **5** YEARS

QUEEN BEE

Every honey bee colony is controlled by a queen bee, who is slightly bigger than the worker bees. She releases a scent called a pheromone that keeps the other bees busy. All the workers are female, but the pheromone stops them breeding on their own account. There are also males called drones, which mate with new queens.

Queen

Worker

Three simple eyes help the bee detect light intensity.

Big compound eyes see well in colour for targeting nectar-bearing flowers.

Antennae detect fragrant flowers, and scents released by other bees.

Front legs have bristly combs for brushing pollen off the body and packing it in the pollen baskets.

"The honey bee beats its wings 250 times a second."

DANCING BEES

When a honey bee comes back from a successful foraging trip, it dances in a special way to tell the other bees where the food was found. This worker bee is performing a "waggle dance", which indicates both the distance of the food source and its direction relative to the Sun.

LIFE STORIES

171

"Just one teaspoon of **honey** is produced by twelve **bees** during their lifetime."

WORKING BEES

Most of the bees in a honey bee colony are non-breeding female workers. The youngest workers feed the bee larvae and make honey. As they get older they turn to cleaning and repairing the honeycomb cells. The oldest workers fly out of the nest or hive to collect nectar and pollen. This young worker is offering liquid food to a hatching drone (male) as he emerges from his nursery cell.

DESERT DRINKER
NAMIB DARKLING BEETLE

This long-legged, ingenious beetle has found a unique way to survive in the dry and desolate Namib Desert of southwest Africa. Here, the only moisture comes from the dense fog that often drifts in from the Atlantic Ocean. Early in the morning, the beetle climbs to the top of a sand dune, uses its long back legs to raise its tail high in the air, and waits. Gradually, the fog forms water droplets on its body, and as these get bigger and heavier they trickle down to its mouth, allowing the beetle to enjoy a much-needed drink.

AT A GLANCE

- **SIZE** 2 cm (¾ in) in length
- **HABITAT** Desert sand dunes
- **LOCATION** Southwest Africa
- **DIET** Wind-blown seeds and plant fragments

STATS AND FACTS

ABOUT

SPECIES

Several darkling beetle species collect water like this; they are all found in the Namib Desert.

ADULT LIFESPAN
3-4
MONTHS

ACTIVE

The beetle is active mainly at night when the desert air cools down.

DEFENCE

Some darkling beetles spray predators with a smelly liquid.

STRATEGY

Some species also dig trenches in the sand to catch rain or fog moisture.

HABITAT
The Namib has less than 10 mm (½ in) of rainfall a year.

PRECIOUS RESOURCE

The tough cuticle (skin) of this desert beetle has a waxy outer layer that stops the insect drying out. It also repels any moisture in the air, but the beetle's handstand technique ensures no water is wasted.

SCUBA-DIVING SPIDER
WATER SPIDER

Spiders cannot breathe underwater, but the water spider has found a way. It carries an air supply in a bubble around its body, enabling the spider to hunt beneath the surface. It even builds an underwater home – a dense, bell-shaped web tied to pond plants that contains a larger air bubble. The spider takes air from the surface to refill the web, but oxygen also enters the bubble from the surrounding water. This is where the spider retreats to eat its prey, while the female spider also uses it as a nursery for her eggs and offspring.

AT A GLANCE

- **SIZE** Up to 18 mm (¾ in) long
- **HABITAT** Ponds, lakes, marshes, and slow-moving streams
- **LOCATION** Europe and northern Asia
- **DIET** Small aquatic animals

STATS AND FACTS

SPECIES

The water spider is unique, with only one species found over a wide area.

LIFESPAN

UP TO
2
YEARS

EGGS

Females lay up to six batches of 50–100 eggs per year.

SPIDERLINGS

After hatching, the young stay in the nest for four weeks before setting up on their own.

DIVING

Water spiders dive deeper to hibernate during the cold winters.

DEFENCE

When threatened, water spiders fight back with a venomous and painful bite.

KILLER CATERPILLAR
LARGE BLUE BUTTERFLY

Some butterflies have a dark secret. The adults are innocent nectar-feeders, but their early lives are spent eating other insects. The large blue is one of many species that prey on ants. The caterpillar tricks a particular type of red ant into carrying it into the ant colony's nest. Here, it spends months feasting on helpless ant larvae before emerging into the sunlight as a winged butterfly.

When the wings are folded, the bright blue of the upper side is hidden.

EARLY DAYS
The female butterfly lays each of her eggs on a wild thyme plant. The tiny caterpillar feeds on the thyme for three weeks, then drops to the ground and produces a sugary liquid, hoping to attract an ant that will carry it off to its nest.

Long, dark-banded antennae detect air movements and scents carried on the breeze.

Big compound eyes enable the butterfly to spot a breeding partner.

The tubular tongue is uncoiled to sip sugary flower nectar.

AT A GLANCE

- **SIZE** Wingspan up to 5 cm (2 in)
- **HABITAT** Sunny slopes with short grass and plenty of wild thyme
- **LOCATION** Europe and northern Asia
- **DIET** Caterpillar eats wild thyme and the larvae of red ants; adult sips nectar

DECEIVER

The caterpillar deceives the ants by acting like one of their own young. It can also release a chemical that mimics the scent of an ant larva, and may even make noises that sound like those made by the ant colony's queen. This fools the ants into looking after their killer guest.

CARRIED AWAY
When the caterpillar has attracted an ant with a sweet-tasting secretion, it starts to behave like an ant larva. This makes the ant pick up the killer caterpillar and carry it back to its nest.

DEADLY GUEST
Once inside the ants' nest, the caterpillar turns into a voracious predator, seizing and eating the ant larvae. After about nine months, the caterpillar turns into a pupa, then becomes a butterfly that crawls out of the nest.

Tiny scales give the wings their colour and pattern.

"Large blues rely on just **one species of ant** for survival."

Winged beauty

The adult large blue is a beautiful butterfly that lives in small colonies and rarely flies far from where it hatched as a caterpillar. It lives for only a few weeks – just long enough to attract a mate and lay eggs.

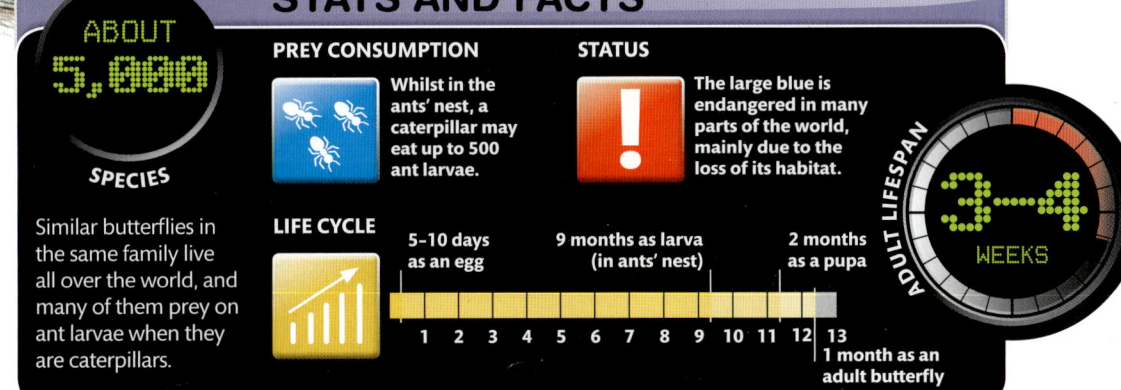

STATS AND FACTS

ABOUT 5,000 SPECIES
Similar butterflies in the same family live all over the world, and many of them prey on ant larvae when they are caterpillars.

PREY CONSUMPTION
Whilst in the ants' nest, a caterpillar may eat up to 500 ant larvae.

STATUS
The large blue is endangered in many parts of the world, mainly due to the loss of its habitat.

LIFE CYCLE
5–10 days as an egg | 9 months as larva (in ants' nest) | 2 months as a pupa

1 2 3 4 5 6 7 8 9 10 11 12 13

1 month as an adult butterfly

ADULT LIFESPAN 3–4 WEEKS

SILK SPINNER
WILD SILK MOTH CATERPILLAR

All moths and butterflies begin life as hungry, soft-bodied caterpillars. In time, each caterpillar becomes a pupa – the stage of life when it transforms into an adult. The pupae are often protected by cocoons of spun silk, and the silk moth in particular produces so much of this valuable fibre that it has become the basis of a huge industry.

Shedding and spinning

The wild silk moth is the ancestor of the domestic silk moth used by the silk industry. The caterpillar uses its powerful jaws to eat voraciously, growing fast and shedding its soft skin four times before spinning the silken cocoon where it turns into a pupa.

Brain

Antenna

NEW THREADS

Silk is produced by many insects and spiders, but the silk moth caterpillar produces far more than most. It is made by the silk glands inside the caterpillar's body, and squeezed out of a spinneret beneath its mouth as a thick, sticky liquid. This solidifies in the air to form two filaments of silk that become glued together as one single thread.

Spinneret

The caterpillar has two clusters of small simple eyes, which cannot see in detail.

There are six true legs at the front, each with a sharp claw.

STATS AND FACTS

ABOUT
150
SPECIES

Silk moths are part of a family of moths that are found all over the world except Europe, and are most common in the tropics.

EGGS

About 500 eggs are produced by a female silk moth in the five days before she dies.

COCOON

It takes a caterpillar 3 days to wrap itself in silk thread, which is about 2,000 m (6,500 ft) long.

YOUNG

Larvae feed constantly on mulberry leaves before reaching full size after about 35 days.

SILK

About 1,000 silkworm cocoons are needed to make enough fabric for one silk shirt.

CATERPILLAR LIFESPAN

45 DAYS

LIFE CYCLE

Silk cloth is made from the silk of the domestic silkworm – a form of the wild silk moth that has been bred to produce as much silk as possible. The caterpillar hatches from an egg and immediately starts feeding on mulberry leaves, its only food source. When fully grown, it makes a cocoon and turns into a moth inside. Eventually, the moth emerges, finds a mate, and the female lays more eggs.

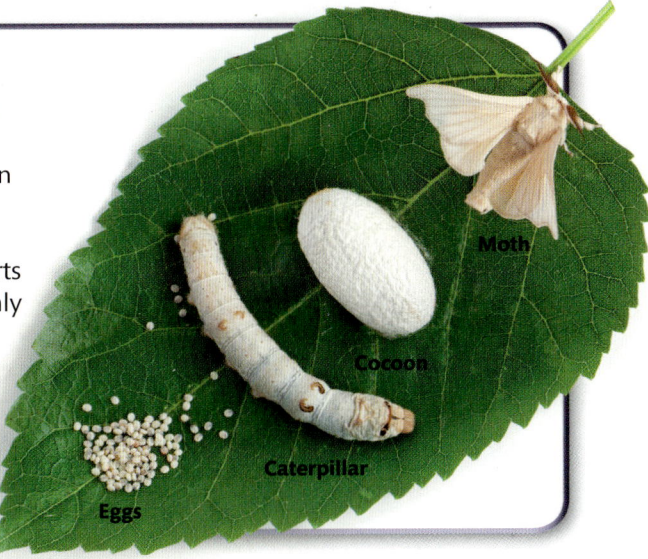

Moth
Cocoon
Caterpillar
Eggs

AT A GLANCE

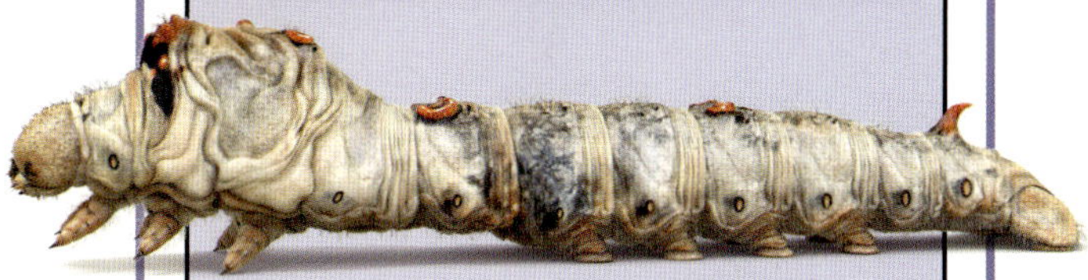

- **SIZE** Caterpillar up to 7.5 cm (3 in) long
- **HABITAT** Woodland
- **LOCATION** East Asia and Japan
- **DIET** Caterpillar eats mulberry leaves; adult does not feed

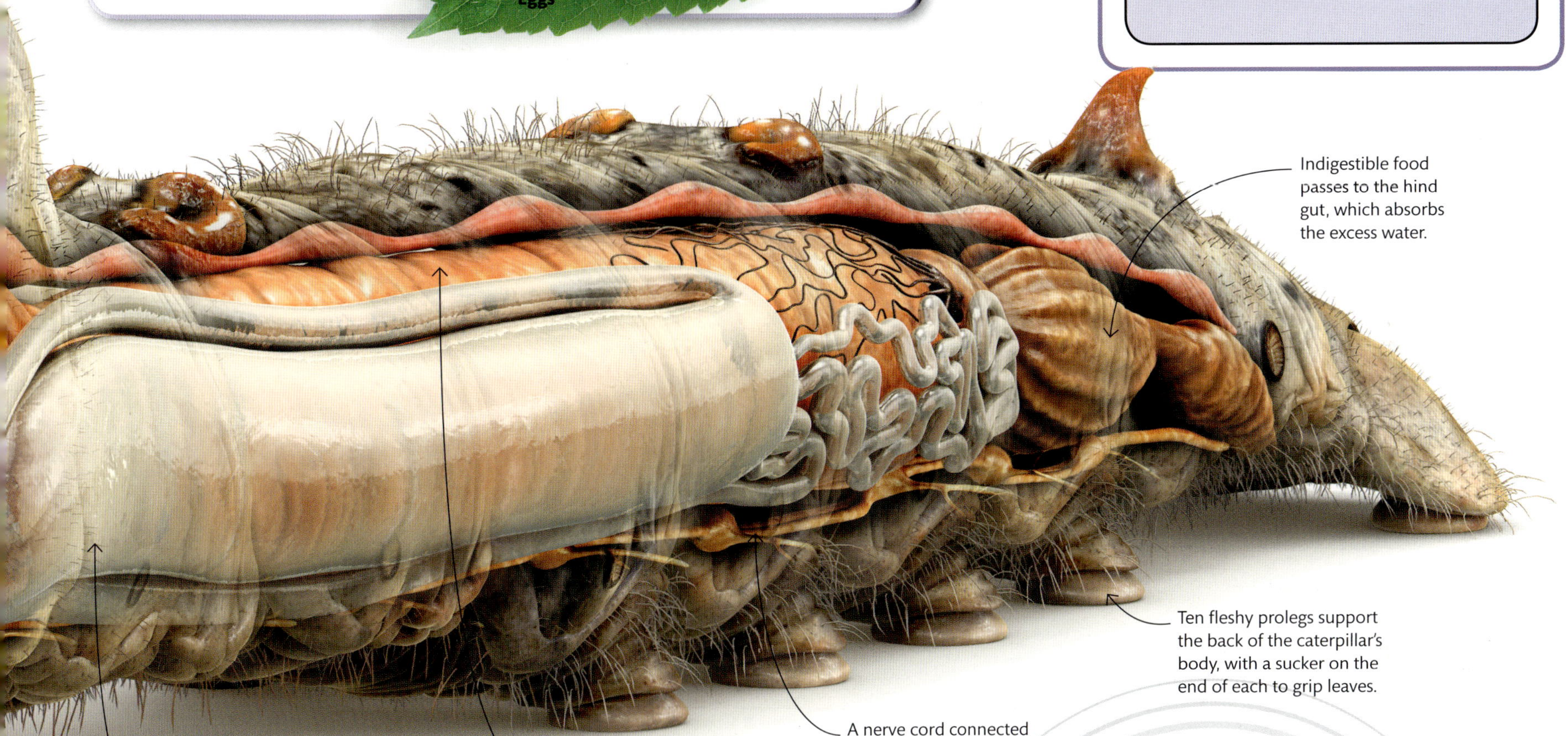
Indigestible food passes to the hind gut, which absorbs the excess water.
Ten fleshy prolegs support the back of the caterpillar's body, with a sucker on the end of each to grip leaves.
A nerve cord connected to the brain extends from head to tail.
Most of the body is filled with a huge mid gut for storing and digesting the caterpillar's leafy food.
Big silk glands, one on each side of the body, produce liquid silk.

SILKWORM'S STORY

Domestic silkworms are reared in trays where they are fed on chopped mulberry leaves. They spin their cocoons inside the trays, resulting in an easy harvest. Then the cocoons are soaked in hot water to soften them, enabling the silk to be unwound on to a spool. Each silk filament is very fine, so up to eight are spun together to form the silk thread that is made into fabric.

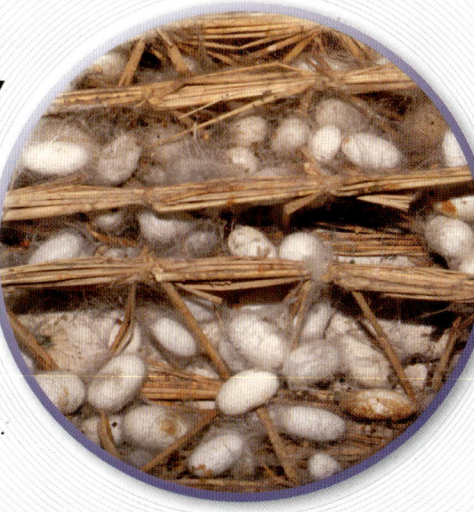

"Cocoons have been harvested for their silk for 5,000 years."

RAIDING PARTY
South American army ants hunt in swarms across the forest floor, attacking and killing anything in their path; they can consume up to 500,000 prey animals a day. Here, a raiding party of worker ants searches for victims, guarded by an extra-large soldier ant with huge, curved jaws.

MARAUDING SWARMS
ARMY ANTS

All ants live in colonies, which usually build permanent nests. But tropical army ants are hunters, and their colonies are so big that they soon run out of prey and have to move to a new patch of forest. They never build a nest. Instead, the workers link limbs to form a living nest of ants called a bivouac. The queen and young live inside this while other workers hunt for food. When the queen is laying eggs the bivouac stays in one place, but when the eggs hatch the whole colony goes on the march again because the hungry larvae need feeding.

AT A GLANCE

- **SIZE** Soldier ants up to 12 mm (½ in) long; worker ants are smaller
- **HABITAT** Tropical rainforest
- **LOCATION** South America
- **DIET** Mainly insects, spiders, scorpions, and sometimes lizards and small mammals

STATS AND FACTS

MORE THAN
200
SPECIES

There are many species of tropical ants that hunt in the same way.

ACTIVITY Army ants have a fixed 35-day activity cycle of breeding and migration.

| days | 5 | 10 | 15 | 20 | 25 | 30 | 35 |

Ant colony moves to a different place every night.

The colony stays in one place when the queen is laying eggs.

SPEED

A raiding party moves at about 20 m (65 ft) per hour.

RAID

The raiding trail can be up to 100 m (330 ft) long and 20 m (65 ft) wide.

WORKER'S LIFESPAN

SEVERAL MONTHS

INSECT ARCHITECTS
PAPER WASPS

Many animals build elaborate, intricate homes but few can match paper wasps for amazing architectural ability. They use paper made from chewed wood pulp to make their nests. Each nest is a cluster of cells containing eggs that hatch as wasp larvae. The wasps feed the larvae until they turn into pupae – the stage when they transform into adults.

AT A GLANCE

- **SIZE** Up to 22 mm (1 in) long
- **HABITAT** Woodland, grassland with trees, and gardens
- **LOCATION** Central America, Caribbean, and southern USA
- **DIET** Insects and nectar

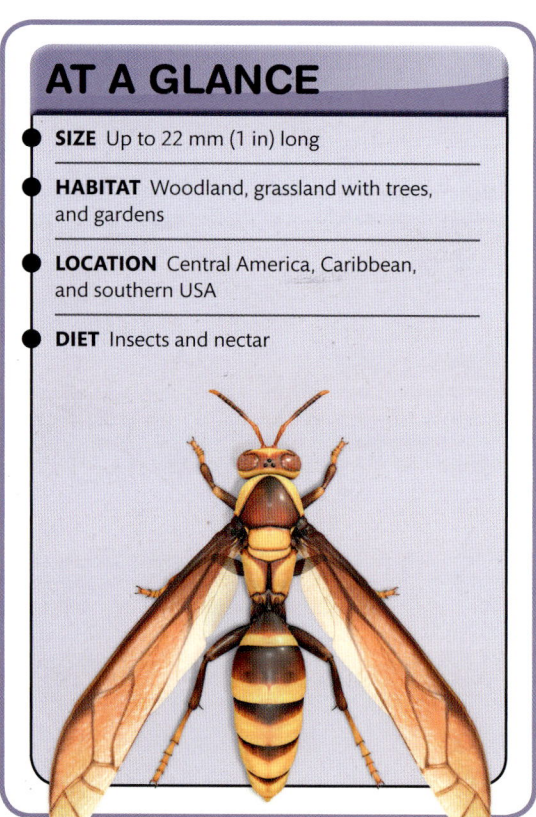

HIDDEN PUPA
Worker wasps feed the legless larvae with chewed-up insects. When the larvae are fully grown, they spin silk caps to seal themselves into their cells. They become wingless pale pupae, which then turn into adult wasps.

An egg is laid by the queen in each cell of the nest.

Building a nest
The queen wasp builds the first few cells of the nest, hanging them from a branch by a slender stalk. When the first workers hatch, they become nest builders, adding extra cells so the queen can lay more eggs. They also gather food and defend the nest with their stings.

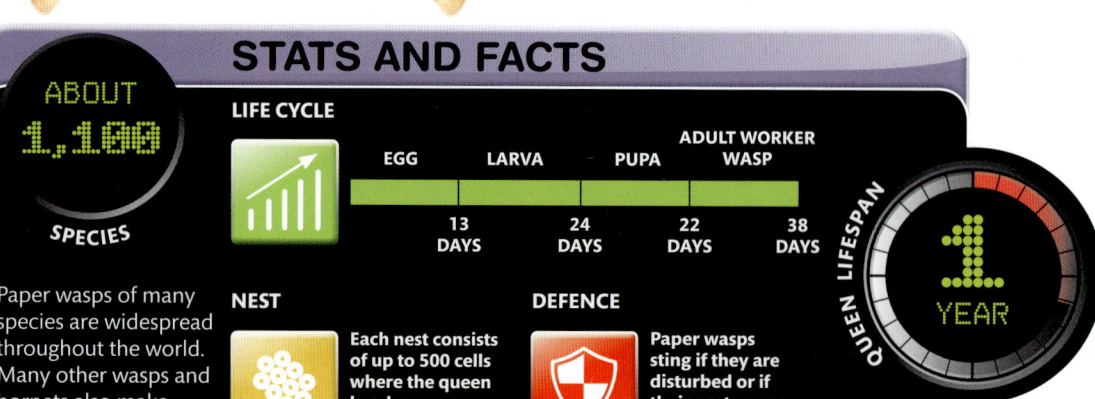

Maggot-like wasp larvae live in open cells.

STATS AND FACTS

ABOUT **1,100** SPECIES

Paper wasps of many species are widespread throughout the world. Many other wasps and hornets also make their nests from paper.

LIFE CYCLE

EGG	LARVA	PUPA	ADULT WORKER WASP
13 DAYS	24 DAYS	22 DAYS	38 DAYS

QUEEN LIFESPAN **1 YEAR**

NEST Each nest consists of up to 500 cells where the queen lays her eggs.

DEFENCE Paper wasps sting if they are disturbed or if their nests come under threat.

Strong stalk is firmly attached to a branch or beam.

The top of the nest is shaped like an umbrella to protect the colony from rain.

Workers are always on guard to defend the nest.

IN FOR THE KILL

The worker wasps supply the colony with food by hunting for caterpillars and other insects. They search bushes and trees near the nest to find prey, which they kill and carry back to the nest. Here, the workers chew the prey into pieces, which they feed to the larvae in their paper cells.

Caps of the pupal cells are made of spun silk.

"Paper wasps **attack** and **sting** anything or anyone that threatens their nest."

KILLER FEATURES

Paper wasps are hunters that use their big compound eyes to seek out insect prey for their queen and her young. They are armed with venomous stings and saw-toothed jaws for killing their victims and cutting them up. Adult wasps cannot eat solid food, but when they feed the prey to the hungry young, they chew it first and swallow some of the juices.

LARGEST COLONY

HITCHING A RIDE

As these leafcutter ant workers carry their pieces of leaf home, smaller workers hitch a lift. They protect the foragers from enemies such as parasitic flies. Meanwhile, much bigger soldier ants defend the nest itself.

FUNGUS FARMERS
LEAFCUTTER ANTS

In the tropical forests of Central America, trees are under constant attack from leafcutter ants. Using their sharp jaws, the ants scissor away pieces of leaf and carry them to their underground nests. But they cannot digest these leaf fragments. Instead, they use them to make a bed of compost for cultivating a fungus. The ants eat this fungus, and feed it to their queen and her young. The system works so well that the nest can support millions of ants, and may grow bigger than a house.

AT A GLANCE

- **SIZE** Workers are 2–14 mm (⅛–½ in) long; the queen is about 22 mm (1 in) long
- **HABITAT** Tropical forests and clearings
- **LOCATION** Mainly Central and South America
- **DIET** Foragers sip leaf sap; all the other ants in the colony eat cultivated fungus

STATS AND FACTS

ABOUT 47 SPECIES

Leafcutter ants live only in the tropical and subtropical parts of the Americas.

QUEEN'S LIFESPAN 14 YEARS

EGGS

The queen ant lays about 150 million eggs during her lifetime.

COLONY

There can be up to 8 million leafcutter ants living in a nest.

NEST SIZE

A mature nest can be as wide as 30 m (100 ft) and as deep as 7 m (20 ft).

STRATEGY

The ants move in long lines, leaving a scent to follow home.

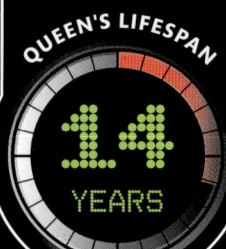

WREAKING HAVOC
DESERT LOCUST

No bug is as destructive as the desert locust. A swarm can strip a whole field bare of vegetation within hours. But locusts do not always wreak havoc like this. Some may spend their entire lives as solitary, harmless insects. They only gather in ravenous swarms if they have multiplied so rapidly that they run out of food.

Adapted for long-distance flying, the wings are longer than the body.

Tubes called tracheae deliver vital oxygen to the internal organs.

Hind gut

Malpighian tubules remove waste substances from the blood.

Swollen ganglia in the main nerve cord in each body segment process nerve signals.

Strong muscles in the long back legs provide the power for hopping.

Eating machine

A locust is a type of grasshopper. It has the same body shape as an ordinary meadow grasshopper, with a pair of long wings and powerful back legs for leaping. Like all grasshoppers it is a plant-eater, and has a large digestive system for processing tough vegetable food.

STATS AND FACTS

ABOUT
12
SWARMING SPECIES

The desert locust is one of a small group of grasshoppers that sometimes change their behaviour to form huge locust swarms.

DISTANCE

Swarms fly up to 130 km a day.

km	50	100	150
miles	31	62	93

EGGS

A female probes the soil with her abdomen, digs a hole and deposits an egg pod containing up to 100 eggs.

YOUNG

Newborn develop through five stages, each bigger than the last.

LIFESPAN
3–5 MONTHS

AT A GLANCE

- **SIZE** Up to 7.5 cm (3 in) long
- **HABITAT** Grasslands and deserts
- **LOCATION** Africa, the Middle East, and southern Asia
- **DIET** Leaves

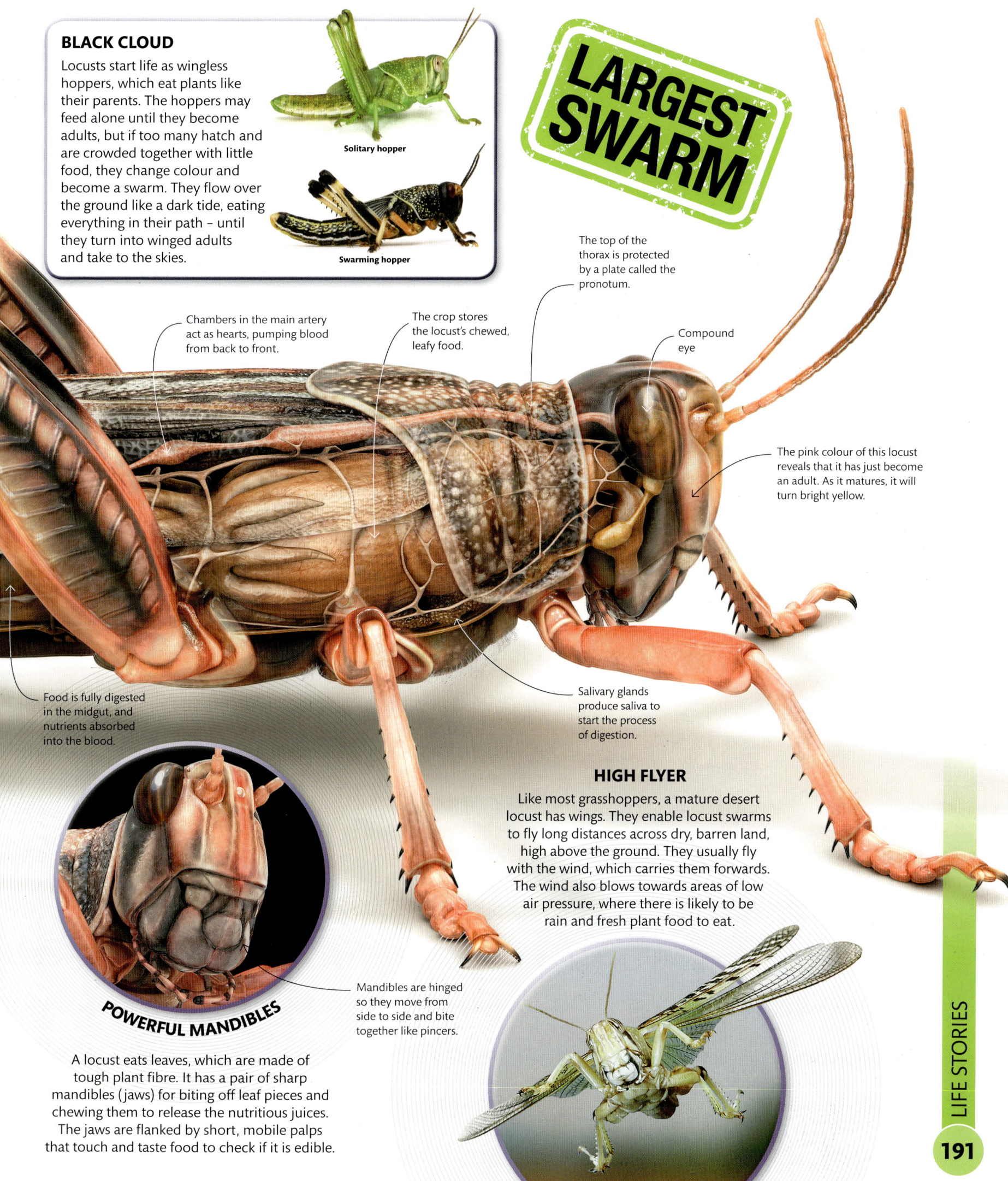

BLACK CLOUD

Locusts start life as wingless hoppers, which eat plants like their parents. The hoppers may feed alone until they become adults, but if too many hatch and are crowded together with little food, they change colour and become a swarm. They flow over the ground like a dark tide, eating everything in their path – until they turn into winged adults and take to the skies.

Solitary hopper

Swarming hopper

LARGEST SWARM

Chambers in the main artery act as hearts, pumping blood from back to front.

The crop stores the locust's chewed, leafy food.

The top of the thorax is protected by a plate called the pronotum.

Compound eye

The pink colour of this locust reveals that it has just become an adult. As it matures, it will turn bright yellow.

Food is fully digested in the midgut, and nutrients absorbed into the blood.

Salivary glands produce saliva to start the process of digestion.

HIGH FLYER

Like most grasshoppers, a mature desert locust has wings. They enable locust swarms to fly long distances across dry, barren land, high above the ground. They usually fly with the wind, which carries them forwards. The wind also blows towards areas of low air pressure, where there is likely to be rain and fresh plant food to eat.

Mandibles are hinged so they move from side to side and bite together like pincers.

POWERFUL MANDIBLES

A locust eats leaves, which are made of tough plant fibre. It has a pair of sharp mandibles (jaws) for biting off leaf pieces and chewing them to release the nutritious juices. The jaws are flanked by short, mobile palps that touch and taste food to check if it is edible.

Locust swarms are rare events, but when they do happen, they can be disastrous. A single swarm can contain billions of hungry locusts, each able to eat their own body weight in food a day. If the swarm settles on a tree, every leaf is eaten, and if the swarm descends on a farm crop, it is completely destroyed. In Africa and Asia, entire harvests have been wiped out by locust swarms, causing catastrophic famines.

"A swarm of desert locusts may contain up to **40 billion members.**"

RIDING HIGH

These baby wolf spiders have just hatched, and are climbing out of the silk egg sac on to their mother's back. They ride with her for about a week until they shed their skin a second time, and can take care of themselves.

BABY BEARER
THIN-LEGGED WOLF SPIDER

Wolf spiders are agile, speedy predators that hunt by sight on the ground. They also rely on their sharp eyes during courtship, because the male tries to attract a female by signalling to her with his big, dark, furry palps. If he succeeds, and they mate, the female carries her eggs with her wherever she goes in a big ball of silk attached to the spinnerets at her tail end. When the baby spiders finally hatch, she carries them around too, until they are able to hunt for themselves.

AT A GLANCE

- **SIZE** About 8 mm (¼ in) long
- **HABITAT** Grassland, woodland, and rocky ground
- **LOCATION** Worldwide
- **DIET** Insects

STATS AND FACTS

ABOUT
500
SPECIES

Small, thin-legged wolf spiders hunt over the ground in suitable habitats all over the world.

LIFESPAN

2-3 YEARS

EGGS

Females heat egg sacs in the sun to boost progress, with 50–100 hatching.

ACTIVE
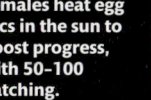
Mostly nocturnal, solitary hunters, but some wait to pounce on passing prey.

FEMALE SPIDER

If the female wolf spider is separated from her egg sac, she will furiously search for it.

DEFENCE

Can deliver a painful bite, but also relies on its camouflage colouring.

SHORTEST LIFESPAN

EYES ON THE PRIZE

A male mayfly has two pairs of compound eyes – one normal pair and a second huge orange pair on top of his head. These extra eyes are for spotting the females as they fly up from the surface of the water to mate.

LIVING FOR THE DAY
MAYFLY

Time is precious for adult mayflies. Some live for just a few minutes, and few survive longer than a day. But the adult stage is only the brief, final chapter of their lives. They live much longer than this as wingless aquatic insects called nymphs, spending years feeding and growing underwater. At the end of their lives, nymphs turn into winged adults that cannot eat at all. Their only purpose is to find a mate and lay their eggs. This takes a few hours – and then, their job done, they die.

AT A GLANCE

- **SIZE** Up to 12 cm (5 in) from head to tail
- **HABITAT** Lakes, rivers, and other fresh water habitats
- **LOCATION** Worldwide except Antarctica
- **DIET** Adults do not eat; aquatic larvae (nymphs) mainly eat vegetable matter, but some are predators

STATS AND FACTS

ABOUT 3,000 SPECIES

Dating back more than 300 million years, mayflies are among the most ancient insects.

ADULT LIFESPAN

TYPICALLY **1-2** DAYS

RECORD BREAKER

The largest mayfly ever, dating from 300 million years ago, had a wingspan of 45 cm.

cm	10	20	30	40	50
in	6		12		18

EGGS

During her short life, the female lays up to 3,000 eggs in water.

DEFENCE

The sheer number of hatching mayflies often overwhelms predators.

PERFECT TIMING
PERIODICAL CICADA

Many insects spend most of their lives hidden away as burrowing larvae. But some species of periodical cicada live underground for 17 years before emerging to live for just a few weeks as winged adults. Amazingly, all the cicadas in the locality appear at once, in the same year, before disappearing for another 17 years until the next mass emergence.

Big muscles inside the thorax power the cicada's large wings.

The body is unusually broad and bulky.

Cicadas have conspicuous, wide-set compound eyes that are very sensitive.

The adult cicada uses its sharp beak to suck sugary plant sap.

Powerful legs are used for climbing.

AT A GLANCE

- **SIZE** About 3 cm (1 in) long
- **HABITAT** Broadleaved forest
- **LOCATION** Eastern USA
- **DIET** Tree sap

STATS AND FACTS

SPECIES

Periodical cicadas live only in the USA, but cicadas that emerge every year live in warm regions throughout the world.

TEMPERATURE

The nymphs emerge from their burrows when the soil temperature is about 17°C (64°F).

EGGS

Each female lays about 500 eggs in batches of 20 before she dies.

EMERGENCE

Up to 370 cicada nymphs come out simultaneously per one sq m (34 per sq ft).

SOUND

The cicada song chorus is louder than a passing motorbike (100 dB).

NYMPH DEVELOPMENT TIME

UP TO 17 YEARS

Remarkable bugs

Billions of periodical cicadas emerge within a day or two of each other on warm spring evenings in North America. They swarm in the trees, then mate, lay their eggs, and die. This mass emergence ensures that many of them survive long enough to breed, because the birds and other local predators cannot eat them all.

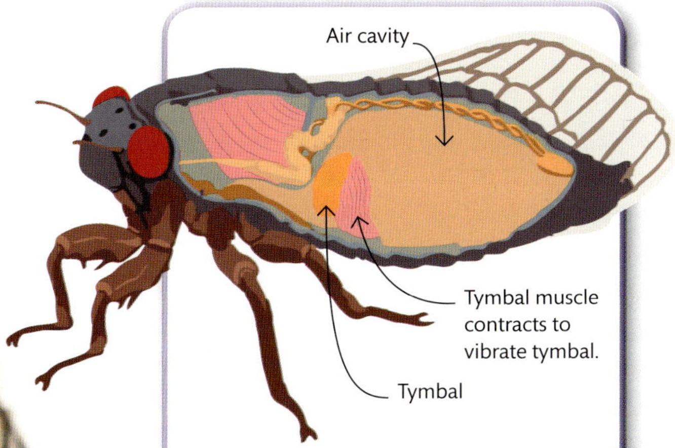

Air cavity

Tymbal muscle contracts to vibrate tymbal.

Tymbal

SINGING BUGS

Male cicadas are equipped with sound-makers called tymbals. They are like tiny drums in each side of the cicada's body. Special muscles pull the tymbals in and then release them to generate a rapid stream of clicks, which is heard as a loud buzzing song. This attracts female cicadas to mate with the males.

The long forewings have stout veins for reinforcement, and a waxy surface that repels water.

Each foot has sharp claws for a firm grip on tree bark.

"The songs of male cicadas are among the loudest insect sounds in the world."

LIKE CLOCKWORK

While some periodical cicadas develop underground for 17 years, others take 13 years. The nymphs grow at the same rate. Eventually, they emerge and clamber on to trees. The males fill the air with their sound to attract females, which lay their eggs on the trees. When the eggs hatch, the nymphs drop to the ground and burrow out of sight for the next 13 or 17 years.

1

BURROWING NYMPH
The cicada nymph spends its long life underground, feeding on the sap from tree roots. When the time finally comes to see daylight, the nymph digs its way to the surface.

2

BREAKING OUT
The dark-coloured nymph climbs on to a tree or plant for its final transformation. It slides out of its old skin for the last time, emerging as a winged adult.

3

STARTING AGAIN
The new adult has a soft body with pale skin. But the skin soon hardens and turns black. The wings expand, enabling the cicada to fly and search for a partner.

LIFE STORIES

NEW BEGINNING

A cicada nymph is stoutly built. When it climbs a tree to shed its skin for the last time, the adult that emerges is very similar apart from colour, and even this will darken with time. But the adult cicada has wings, unlike the nymph. The wings are small and crumpled at first, but this cicada will soon start pumping fluid into the wing veins to make them unfurl and expand.

PATERNAL PROTECTION
GIANT WATER BUG

Most insects abandon their eggs once they are laid. But some giant water bugs are different, because the female carefully glues her eggs to the back of the male. He then carries the eggs until they hatch to ensure predators do not eat his offspring. Each young water bug turns into a fierce predator that attacks insects, frogs, and fish. Using its powerful, grasping front legs to impale the victim, the bug stabs it with its sharp beak to inject a paralysing, flesh-dissolving saliva so that it can suck up and digest the meal.

AT A GLANCE

- **SIZE** Up to 10 cm (4 in) from head to tail
- **HABITAT** Lakes, rivers, and other fresh waters
- **LOCATION** North America, South America, Africa, Australia, India, and Southeast Asia
- **DIET** Any freshwater animals they can catch

STATS AND FACTS

ABOUT
160
SPECIES

Giant water bugs mainly live in warmer parts of the world, but some live as far north as Canada.

LIFESPAN

UP TO **1** YEAR

EGGS A female lays 100 or more eggs in one batch.

DEFENCE If threatened, the defensive strategy is bite back or play dead.

LIGHT BUGS Also known as electric light bugs because they are attracted to night lights.

FOOD In some parts of Southeast Asia, water bugs are considered a delicacy.

GLOSSARY

ABDOMEN
The rear part of an animal's body, containing the digestive organs.

ANAESTHETIC
A substance that numbs pain. Some insects inject an anaesthetic when they bite, so the victim feels nothing.

ANTENNAE
A pair of long, movable sense organs (feelers) used to detect movement and chemicals in the air.

AQUATIC
Living in water. Aquatic bugs include water beetles and water spiders. Some insects, such as dragonflies and mayflies, are aquatic in their early stages but surface and fly as adults.

ARACHNID
An animal such as a spider or scorpion with pincer-like mouthparts and four pairs of legs.

ARTHROPOD
An animal with an external skeleton, jointed legs, and no backbone. Arthropods include insects, spiders, and crustaceans like lobsters and crabs.

CAMOUFLAGE
Colours or shapes that make something hard to see against its background. Camouflage provides protection from predators, but can also hide a hunter. Some insects look just like the leaves, flowers, or twigs that they live on.

CARRION
The dead and rotting flesh of an animal, which is important food for many bugs.

CATERPILLAR
The soft-bodied, wingless, and immature form of a butterfly or moth.

CHELICERAE
The jaw-like mouthparts of a spider, scorpion, or similar arachnid.

CHITIN
The substance that forms the tough external skeleton of an arthropod.

COCOON
A protective enclosure made by an animal, typically using silk.

COLONY
A group of animals or other organisms that live together. Ants and bees are bugs that live in large colonies.

COMPOUND EYES
The main eyes of adult insects and some other animals, made up of hundreds of elements, each with its own tiny lens.

COURTSHIP
Behaviour designed to attract the attention of a breeding partner, such as showing off coloured wings.

CROP
Part of the digestive system, used for storing food that has just been swallowed.

CUTICLE
The outer protective skin of an arthropod. It is typically made of a tough material and forms an exoskeleton.

DORMANT
Inactive, as though sleeping. Many bugs have a dormant period in their development stage. This saves their energy and helps them to survive very cold or dry weather.

ELYTRA
Adapted forewings that form the tough wing cases of a beetle. Elytra provide protective covering for the delicate hind wings that are used for flying.

ENZYME
A protein substance that accelerates a chemical reaction, such as the digestive enzymes a spider injects into its prey to break down the body tissues.

EXOSKELETON
The tough external skeleton of an animal such as an insect. Also known as the cuticle.

FANGS
Sharp, hollow tooth-like structures. Many arthropods, including spiders, inject venom through their fangs to kill or paralyse their prey.

FERTILIZE
To bring male and female cells together so that they develop into seeds or eggs. Many insects play an important role in plant fertilization by carrying pollen from the male to the female parts of flowers.

FORCIPULES
Sharp-tipped, claw-like front limbs used by centipedes to inject venom and kill prey.

FOREWINGS
An insect's front pair of wings.

FOSSIL
The remains or traces of any living thing that survive decay and are often preserved by being turned to stone.

GLAND
A small organ in the body that makes and releases a chemical substance, such as hormones, saliva, or silk.

GRUB
A soft-bodied insect larva.

HABITAT
A place where wildlife lives.

HALTERES
Tiny drumstick-shaped organs seen in all true flies. They beat with the wings and help the insect to stay balanced in flight.

HIND WINGS
Rear pair of wings.

HONEYDEW
A sweet-tasting, sticky waste produced by some insects that feed on sugary plant sap.

INSECT
An arthropod that has three pairs of legs when adult, and often has one or two pairs of wings.

INVERTEBRATE
An animal that does not have a jointed internal skeleton.

IRIDESCENT
Glittering with colour created by the way sunlight reflects from a textured surface. The effect may be seen on a butterfly's wings or a shiny beetle.

LARVA
The young form of an insect, which looks very different from the adult. Larvae (plural) include moth and butterfly caterpillars, fly maggots, and beetle and wasp grubs.

LIFE CYCLE
The stages through which an animal passes to reach its adult form and be capable of reproducing.

MALPIGHIAN TUBULES
Small tubes that gather waste chemicals from the body fluids of arthropods.

MANDIBLES
Sharp jaw-like structures used for biting and chewing.

MEMBRANE
A thin sheet of material, such as the wing of a flying insect.

MICROBE
A microscopic living thing.

MIGRATION
The movement of a population from one place to another. Many animals migrate at certain times of year to find warmer weather, more food, or the right breeding conditions.

MOLECULE
A tiny particle of something formed from a fixed number of atoms.

MOULT
The shedding of a bug's cuticle. A new soft cuticle beneath expands and hardens. This lets the animal grow, which is impossible inside a hard case. Moults may be repeated several times.

MYRIAPOD
An animal such as a centipede or millipede with nine or more pairs of legs.

NECTAR
Sugar solution produced by flowers to attract animals.

NOCTURNAL
Active at night. Bugs that come out after dark include moths, fireflies, cockroaches, mosquitoes, and spiders.

NUTRIENTS
Substances obtained from food that living things use for energy and growth.

NYMPH
A young form of an insect that is similar to the adult, but wingless. Nymphs moult several times before becoming fully mature.

OCELLI
Simple eyes that are used to detect light intensity.

OVIPOSITOR
A tube or hollow blade used for laying eggs.

PALPS
Short limb-like structures near the mouth, usually for handling food.

PARASITE
A living thing that lives on or inside the body of another live organism, feeding on it without killing it.

PHEROMONE
A special scent that carries a message to other animals of the same species. This may be used for such purposes as marking a trail or attracting a mate.

POLLEN
Tiny grains produced by flowers. These contain the male cells needed to fertilize female cells and make them develop into seeds.

POLLINATION
The process of delivering pollen to the female structures of a flower. Many insects are useful pollinators.

PREDATOR
An animal that kills other animals for food.

PREY
An animal eaten by another animal.

PROTEIN
An organic, nitrogen-containing compound. Proteins are essential to all living organisms, and are used for making enzymes and body tissues.

PUPA
The stage during the life cycle of some insects when a larva such as a caterpillar turns into an adult such as a butterfly. (Plural: pupae.)

QUEEN
An egg-laying female in a colony of social insects such as bees or ants. A queen is bigger and longer-lived than her companions.

RAINFOREST
A forest in a warm region of the world where there is high annual rainfall.

SALIVA
Fluid produced by salivary glands that starts the process of digestion.

SCRUBLAND
An area of land where there is a mixture of low-growing plants such as bushes and grasses.

SILK
A strong, elastic material produced by spiders to make webs and by some insects to make cocoons.

SPECIES
A scientific grouping of animals that all look alike and can mate with one another to produce young. Animals of different species cannot pair up.

SPINNERET
A nozzle on a bug's body that produces silk. Spiders have several spinnerets.

SPIRACLES
Breathing holes in a bug's outer skeleton through which air is taken in and carbon dioxide is expelled.

STYLET
A slender blade with a sharp tip that forms part of the mouthparts of some bugs and is used for piercing.

SUBTROPICAL
Describing zones where the climate is not as hot and wet as in tropical regions but warmer than in temperate (moderate) zones.

THORAX
The central part of an insect's body, to which its legs and wings are attached.

TISSUE
In an animal or plant, a collection of cells that together form living material such as muscle and skin.

TOXIN
Another word for poison.

TRACHEAE
A network of tubes that carry air to the muscles and organs of the body.

TROPICAL
Describes a region close to the equator. A tropical climate is typically very hot and humid.

TRUE BUG
A scientific term for a group of insects with special features, including mouthparts for stabbing and sucking. Pondskaters, cicadas, and froghoppers are all true bugs.

VENOM
Poison that a biting or stinging animal uses for hunting or defence.

WORKER
A non-reproducing member of an insect colony, usually female. Workers perform specialized tasks, such as gathering food and nest-building.

Abbreviations used in this book	
/	per – for example, km/h means kilometres per hour
°C	degrees Celsius
cm	centimetre
dB	decibel
°F	degrees Fahrenheit
ft	foot
g	gram
in	inch
kg	kilogram
km	kilometre
lb	pound
m	metre
min	minute
mm	millimetre
mph	miles per hour
oz	ounce
sec	second
sq	square

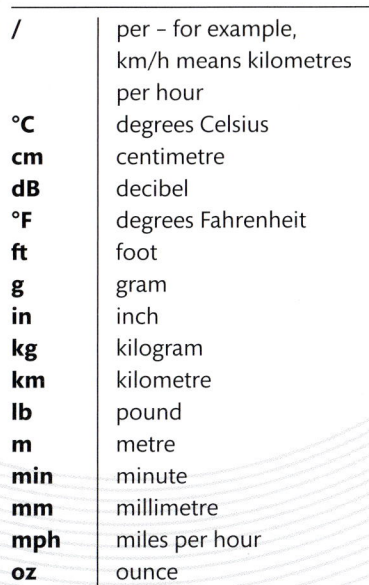

INDEX

ACKNOWLEDGMENTS

Dorling Kindersley would like to thank: Anjana Nair, Amit Varma, and Charvi Arora for design assistance; Surya Sarangi for additional picture research; Steve Crozier for retouching; Bharti Bedi for editorial assistance; Jane Evans for proofreading; and Carron Brown for the index.

Picture Credits
The publisher would like to thank the following for their kind permission to reproduce their photographs:

(Key: a-above; b-below/bottom; c-centre; f-far; l-left; r-right; t-top)

4 Corbis: Wouter Pattyn/Buiten-beeld/Minden Pictures (cra). **Nicky Bay:** (ca). **5 Ireneusz Irass Waledzik:** (cla). **Thomas Marent:** (ca). **6 Ryan Jayawardena:** (bl). **6-7 Science Photo Library:** Gilles Mermet. **7 Alexander Hyde:** (crb). **Thomas Marent:** (br). **Nicky Bay:** (tr). **Igor Siwanowicz:** (cra). **8 Nicky Bay:** (clb). **Alex Wild/myrmecos.net:** (bl). **9 OceanwideImages.com:** (crb). **10 Alexander Hyde:** (br). **Dreamstime.com:** Pzaxe (tr). **11 123RF.com:** Cosmin Manci (cb); Parmoht Hongtong (tr). **Dreamstime.com:** Amwu (cl). **13 Dreamstime.com:** Alessandrozocc (bc). **Getty Images:** Stephen Dalton (tr). **Melvyn Yeo:** (cr). **14-15 naturepl.com:** Alex Hyde. **16 Alamy Images:** Survivalphotos (tl). **Brian Parsons:** (bc). **naturepl.com:** Alex Hyde (ca). **Nicky Bay:** (tr, ftr). **16-17 Corbis:** Ingo Arndt/Minden Pictures (c). **Dreamstime.com:** Stevenrussellsmithphotos (cb). **17 Getty Images:** Laura Berman/Design Pics (tr). **Nicky Bay:** (ftl, tl, tc, tc/soft cuticle). **21 naturepl.com:** Nature Production (cra). **22 Dreamstime.com:** Mgkuijpers. **23 Corbis:** Wolfgang Kaehler (cr). **24-25 Dreamstime.com:** Mgkuijpers. **25 naturepl.com:** MYN/Andrew Snyder (cr). **26 Science Photo Library:** Jerzy Gubernator (cb). **27 FLPA:** Ingo Arndt/Minden Pictures (cb). **Photoshot:** Adrian Hepworth (cra). **Science Photo Library:** Dirk Wiersma (tc). **28-29 naturepl.com:** Philippe Clement. **29 Dreamstime.com:** Henriklh (cr). **30 Masterfile:** Minden Pictures (c). **30-31 Rod Morris Productions. 32 Dorling Kindersley:** Natural History Museum, London (cb). **32-33 naturepl.com:** Steven David Miller. **34 Corbis:** Dennis Kunkel Microscopy, Inc./Visuals Unlimited (cl). **34-35 Nicky Bay. 35 123RF.com:** Dmitry Knorre (tr). **naturepl.com:** Jan Hamrsky (br). **36 SuperStock:** Universal Images Group (br). **38-39 Getty Images:** Thunderbolt_TW (Bai Heng-yao) photography. **40-41 naturepl.com:** Nature Production. **41 Dreamstime.com:** Isselee (crb).

42 OceanwideImages.com: (cl). **42-43 OceanwideImages.com. 44-45 SuperStock:** Minden Pictures. **45 SuperStock:** Minden Pictures (cr). **46-47 Igor Siwanowicz. 47 naturepl.com:** Robert Thompson (cr). **48-49 SuperStock:** Imagemore (c). **49 123RF.com:** Eric Isselee (cr). **Fotolia:** Eric Isselee (tr). **naturepl.com:** Jabruson (br). **Science Photo Library:** Patrick Landmann (bc). **50-51 naturepl.com:** Kim Taylor. **53 Christian Kronmuller:** (tl). **54-55 Alamy Images:** Living Levels Photography. **55 Alex Wild/myrmecos.net:** (cr). **56-57 Nicky Bay. 57 Nicky Bay:** (cr). **58-59 Nicky Bay. 59 Nicky Bay:** (cr). **60 Corbis:** Ingo Arndt/Minden Pictures (cl). **60-61 Lukas Jonaitis. 62-63 Igor Siwanowicz. 62 Corbis:** Solvin Zankl/Visuals Unlimited (c). **naturepl.com:** Kim Taylor (cl). **63 Alamy Images:** Arto Hakola (crb); Xunbin Pan (cra). **Corbis:** Mark Moffett/Minden Pictures (br). **Dorling Kindersley:** Thomas Marent (tr). **64 Kurt- orionmystery.blogspot.com:** (cl). **64-65 Kurt- orionmystery.blogspot.com. 66-67 Science Photo Library:** Dr Harold Rose. **67 Hisako Ricketts:** (cr). **69 SuperStock:** Minden Pictures (tl). **70 Science Photo Library:** Barbara Strnadova (c). **70-71 Masterfile:** Minden Pictures. **74-75 National Geographic Creative. 75 Alamy Images:** Greg C. Grace (cr). **76 Alamy Images:** The Natural History Museum (cl). **76-77 SuperStock:** Biosphoto. **77 naturepl.com:** Simon Colmer (cr). **Science Photo Library:** AMI Images (bc). **78 Alamy Images:** Bob Gibbons (crb). **Warren Photographic Limited:** (bc). **79 Nicky Bay:** (crb). **80 Dreamstime.com:** Earlydawnphotography (clb). **Jurgen Otto:** (br). **Warren Photographic Limited:** (cl). **80-81 123RF.com:** Noppharat Prathumthip. **81 Alan Henderson:** (tc). **82-83 Thomas Shahan. 84-85 naturepl.com:** Rolf Nussbaumer. **85 FLPA:** Cisca Castelijns, NiS/Minden Pictures (cr). **86 Nicky Bay/National Geographic Creative** (clb). **86-87 Dreamstime.com:** Sergej Kondratenko. **87 123RF.com:** Song Qiuju (tr). **Ashok Captain:** (cl). **88-89 Roy Anderson. 89 naturepl.com:** Kim Taylor (cr). **90-91 Svatoslav Vrabec. 92 Science Photo Library:** Eye of Science (tl, bc); Steve Gschmeissner (tc). **92-93 Science Photo Library:** Eye of Science (c). **93 Science Photo Library:** John Walsh (tr). **94 Corbis:** Jef Meul/NiS/Minden Pictures (cl). **94-95 Corbis:** Jef Meul/NiS/Minden Pictures. **96-97 Nicky Bay. 97 Corbis:** Paul Starosta (crb). **98 Alamy Images:** dpa picture alliance (cl). **99 Science Photo Library:** Power and Syred (tr); Steve Gschmeissner (crb). **100-101 Alamy Images:** Brian Hewitt. **104 Nicky Bay:** (cl).

104-105 OceanwideImages.com. 106 naturepl.com: Rod Clarke/John Downer Produ (bc). **106-107 Nicky Bay. 107 naturepl.com:** Alex Hyde (tr). **Science Photo Library:** Alex Hyde (ca). **108-109 Thomas Shahan. 109 Dreamstime.com:** Stig Karlsson (cr). **110-111 FLPA:** Â © Biosphoto, Roger Dauriac/Biosphoto. **111 Getty Images:** Amanda Sweet/EyeEm (c). **112-113 Nicky Bay. 114-115 Corbis:** Alex Hyde/Nature Picture Library. **115 Alamy Images:** Life on white (bc); Nature Picture Library (tl). **Igor Siwanowicz:** (cb, c, ca, tc). **116 Photoshot:** James Carmichael Jr (cl). **116-117 John Flannery. 118-119 FLPA:** Photo Researchers. **119 naturepl.com:** Barry Mansell (cr). **120 Corbis:** Michael Durham/Minden Pictures (cl). **120-121 FLPA:** Chien Lee/Minden Pictures. **122 123RF.com:** Christian Musat (cl). **122-123 Corbis:** Wouter Pattyn/Buiten-beeld/Minden Pictures. **124-125 Alamy Images:** Robert Shantz (cl). **125 Alamy Images:** Robert Hamm (cr). **127 Dreamstime.com:** Artjazz (br). **128-129 FLPA:** ImageBroker. **130-131 Robert Suter. 131 Alamy Images:** Hemis (cr). **132 Alamy Images:** Robert HENNO (cl). **132-133 Igor Siwanowicz. 133 Dreamstime.com:** Catalinc (crb). **Jan Hamrsky:** (cb); **134-135 Alex Wild/myrmecos.net. 135 D. Magdalena Sorger:** (cr). **136 Photoshot:** NHPA (cl). **137 Science Photo Library:** Natural History Museum, London (crb). **V.Trailin:** (cra). **140 FLPA:** Konrad Wothe/Minden Pictures (cl). **140-141 Ireneusz Irass Waledzik. 142 Dreamstime.com:** Tzooka (cl). **142-143 Igor Siwanowicz. 143 Alamy Images:** imageBROKER (bc/Burnet moth). **FLPA:** Photo Researchers (br). **Getty Images:** Danita Delimont (bl). **Mark Moore, Moore Live Images:** (tr). **Science Photo Library:** Dr Jeremy Burgess (bc). **144 Alamy Images:** Photosampler (crb); Scott Camazine (cl). **144-145 MacroscopicSolutions. 145 Corbis:** David Scharf (tc). **Science Photo Library:** Cloud Hill Imaging Ltd. (crb); Natural History Museum, London (cra); Power and Syred (br). **146 Alex Wild/myrmecos.net:** (cl). **146-147 Alex Wild/myrmecos.net. 147 Alamy Images:** age fotostock (tr). **Michael Doe:** (tl). **Rodrigo Viveros Agusto:** (crb). **SuperStock:** Animals Animals (cra). **W. Wuster:** (br). **148 Science Photo Library:** Steve Gschmeissner (cl). **149 Alamy Images:** Stocktrek Images, Inc. (crb). **Warren Photographic Limited:** (br). **150 naturepl.com:** Daniel Heuclin (cl). **150-151 naturepl.com:** Daniel Heuclin. **152 Alex Wild/myrmecos.net:** (cl). **152-153 123RF.com:** Mr.Smith Chetanachan. **153 FLPA:** Gerard Lacz

(tc/Hissing cockroach). **Masterfile:** Minden Pictures (tc). **Nicky Bay:** (crb, tr). **156 Photoshot:** M I Walker/NHPA (clb). **156-157 naturepl.com:** Alex Hyde. **157 Alamy Images:** The Natural History Museum (tl). **FLPA:** Jeremy Early (tr). **158 SuperStock:** imageBROKER (cl). **158-159 Svatoslav Vrabec. 161 David Gould/naturespot.org.uk:** (bc). **Dreamstime.com:** Nolte Lourens (bl). **162-163 Mark Leppin. 163 Ron Hay, Greater Napanee, Canada- www.megapixeltravel.com:** (cr). **164 Corbis:** Peter Johnson (clb); Radius Images (c). **165 Corbis:** Anthony Bannister/Gallo Images (br). **Getty Images:** Mark Moffett (tc). **166-167 Corbis:** Ch'ien Lee/Minden Pictures. **168 Getty Images:** arlindo71 (cl). **168-169 Hubert Polacek. 170 Alamy Images:** Phil Degginger (clb). **Ardea:** Steve Hopkin (cl). **170-171 Dreamstime.com:** Isselee (c). **171 Corbis:** Paul Starosta (cra). **172-173 Alex Wild/myrmecos.net. 174 Getty Images:** Mark Moffett (cl). **174-175 Ardea:** Karl Terblanche. **176 Alamy Images:** imageBROKER (cl). **176-177 Getty Images:** Robert F. Sisson. **178 Alamy Images:** Paul R. Sterry/Nature Photographers Ltd (bl). **Peter Eeles/UK Butterflies:** (c). **178-179 Corbis:** Michel Gunther/Copyright : www.biosphoto.com/Biosphoto. **179 Ardea:** John Mason (ca). **National Geographic Creative:** (c). **181 Corbis:** Christophe Loviny (bc). **Getty Images:** baobao ou (tc). **182-183 Photoshot:** K. Wothe. **183 Dreamstime.com:** Ryszard Laskowski (cr). **185 Judy Gallagher:** (tr). **186-187 Dusan Beno. 188-189 Corbis:** Mark Moffett/Minden Pictures. **189 Robert Harding Picture Library:** Konrad Wothe (cl). **191 The American Association for the Advancement of Science:** Steve Rogers (cla); Tom Fayle (tc). **Warren Photographic Limited:** (bc). **192-193 naturepl.com:** Mike Potts. **194-195 Nicky Bay. 195 Getty Images:** David Chambon Photographie (cl). **196-197 Rex Shutterstock:** F1 Online. **197 Nicky Bay:** (c). **198 Alamy Images:** Jim Lane (cl). **198-199 Alex Wild/myrmecos.net. 199 Alamy Images:** B. Mete Uz (bc, bc/Breaking Out). **Corbis:** Mitsuhiko Imamori/Minden Pictures (c). **200-201 Thomas Marent. 202-203 naturepl.com:** Nature Production. **204 Corbis:** Alex Hyde/Nature Picture Library (tr). **206 Alamy Images:** Living Levels Photography (tr). **FLPA:** Â © Biosphoto, Roger Dauriac/Biosphoto (tc); ImageBroker (ftr). **208 SuperStock:** Minden Pictures (tr)

All other images © Dorling Kindersley
For further information see:
www.dkimages.com